# ESSENTIAL ACCOUNTING FOR MANAGERS

# ESSENTIAL ACCOUNTING FOR MANAGERS

A. P. ROBSON

B.SC.(ECON.), F.C.A., F.C.M.A.

*Professor of Management Accounting,*
*Cranfield School of Management*

CASSELL LONDON

CASSELL LIMITED
35 Red Lion Square, London WC1R 4SG
and at Sydney, Auckland, Toronto, Johannesburg,
an affiliate of Macmillan Publishing Co. Inc.,
New York

First published 1966
Second edition 1967
Third edition 1970
Fourth edition 1979
Second impression 1980

I.S.B.N. 0 304 30385 2

Printed in Great Britain by Richard Clay,
(The Chaucer Press), Ltd., Bungay, Suffolk

TO
JOYCE AND ANDREW

# PREFACE TO THE FIRST EDITION

*Essential Accounting for Managers* has been written for the non-accountant manager. It is the outcome of several years' experience at Ashridge Management College, company training centres and at the B.I.M. Oxford Course in Management Practice. The book has been written in the belief that every manager needs to equip himself with a basic knowledge of accounting; particularly in order to make informed decisions, and to see the effect of his actions, or intended actions, on the financial position and profitability of his company. Only those aspects of accounting which are considered relevant for this purpose have been included, so that the book aims to improve managerial performance, rather than to provide a miscellany of background reading on financial topics.

Accounting is seen as a useful aid to management at successive stages, from the analysis of a business situation, through the planning of operations and projects, to a comparison of performance with plan, the whole being carried out in an environment of change. Explanations of how figures are calculated are given at intervals throughout the book, in sufficient detail to enable the manager to understand, and make proper use of, the techniques under discussion. A chapter on more general aspects of accounting measurement is also provided. Throughout the book, detailed calculations of little value to the user of accounting have been avoided.

In this way it is intended that the book will provide a basic understanding of those essential aspects of accounting which will be of value to a wide variety of managers in their contact with accountants and accounting reports in practice. The book will also be of interest to management teachers and training officers, who are responsible for the accounting aspects of management courses, or who are running intensive appreciation courses in accounting for non-financial managers.

I would like to thank Alan Johnson, B.A., A.C.W.A., of Ashridge Management College, and Antony Hichens, M.B.A., B.A., Barrister at Law, of the Rio Tinto-Zinc Corporation, both of whom read a section of the typescript and made a number of helpful comments and suggestions. I would also like to thank Miss Joan Elliott for the unfailing speed and accuracy with which she typed the initial drafts and the final text.

*Whitchurch-on-Thames,* 1966          A. P. ROBSON

vii

# PREFACE TO THE FOURTH EDITION

Since this book was first written (1966) many countries of the world have experienced significant rates of inflation, as a result of which new approaches to accounting have been and are being developed. In addition, it is noticeable that changes have taken place in the use of modern approaches to project evaluation.

In the light of these developments, I have made some alterations to the text, notably in Chapters 3 and 4. However, the basic structure and style of the original book has been retained, as *Essential Accounting for Managers* seems to have met the needs of a large number of practising managers in many parts of the world.

The object of the book remains as before: to provide a basic understanding of those essential aspects of accounting which will be of value to a wide variety of managers in their contact with accountants and accounting reports in practice.

Philomena Sutherland and Filomena Martignetti typed the re-drafts for this edition: my thanks to them both for an excellent job.

*Berkhamsted*, 1978                                          A. P. ROBSON

# CONTENTS

# 1 ANALYSING A BUSINESS

In order to analyse a business situation a manager may turn to the balance sheet, which is one form in which the accountant presents a number of significant facts about a business in figures. A balance sheet is a snapshot picture of a business showing its financial position at a point in time, and, properly interpreted, can provide a manager with a good deal of useful information. The balance sheet is a convenient starting point for analysis, which may lead to a better understanding of the strengths and weaknesses, not only of a business as a whole, but of its individual sections as well. A broad understanding of the contents of a balance sheet, and the type of analysis which might flow from it, also enables individual managers to see more clearly the effect of their actions on the financial position of a business and on its profitability.

This chapter will explain the general framework of a balance sheet by considering first of all a simple case of a private individual who wants to assess his own financial position. This will not only emphasize the basic simplicity of the balance sheet framework, but will also enable managers to obtain a quicker understanding of balance sheets found in business life, of the meaning of terms used, and of the ratios and comparisons which may be prepared for them by their accountants.

*Assets*

Let us take as a first illustration the case of an individual, J. B., who asks himself the question: "What method could I adopt to summarize my own financial position?" J. B. might approach this problem by writing out a list of things that he owns. A simple list could be as follows:

J. B.
WHAT I OWN
*1st January*
House
Furniture
Car
Cash at bank

J. B. now puts a money figure to these items. Let us assume that he has £500 in the bank, and that he lists his house, furniture and car at their cost price, i.e. at the sum of money which had to be provided in the first place to enable him to acquire these items.

J. B.
WHAT I OWN
1st January

| | £ |
|---|---|
| House, cost | 40,000 |
| Furniture, cost | 10,000 |
| Car, cost | 8,000 |
| Cash at bank | 500 |
| Total | £58,500 |

This is a list of J. B.'s assets: a list of valuable things that J. B. owns, which have been acquired at a measurable cost.

*Sources of Finance*

Having drawn up such a list, it would be logical for J. B. to ask another question: "Who is financing these assets and by how much?" J. B. now requires a second list showing his various sources of finance. Suppose that, at 1st January, a building society is lending him £25,000 towards the cost of the house. This is a source of finance which is in addition to the money J. B. has himself put into the house out of his own capital. J. B. has put in £15,000 out of his own capital (the difference between the cost of the house, £40,000, and the building society loan of £25,000).

Suppose also that J. B. has recently acquired £700 worth of furniture, which he has not yet paid for. He has an account at the furniture shop, so that the shop is in fact currently financing £700 of the total cost of his furniture. The remaining £9,300 has been paid for by J. B. out of his own capital.

To complete the picture, let us also assume that the money for the car, £8,000, and the money J. B. has in the bank, £500, have both come out of his own capital, i.e. at 1st January J. B. does not require to borrow any money or raise any additional outside source of finance to enable him to own these assets. J. B.'s second list, showing his sources of finance, therefore reads as follows:

J. B.
SOURCES OF FINANCE
*1st January*

|  |  | £ |
|---|---|---|
| J. B.—Own capital | (for house) | 15,000 |
|  | (for furniture) | 9,300 |
|  | (for car) | 8,000 |
|  | (for bank account) | 500 |
|  | Total | 32,800 |
| Building society loan |  | 25,000 |
| Furniture shop |  | 700 |
|  | Total £58,500 | |

## The Balance Sheet

If we put these two lists, assets and sources of finance, on one statement, we have a balance sheet showing J. B.'s financial position at a point in time, in this case 1st January.

J. B.
BALANCE SHEET
*1st January*

| Sources of Finance | £ | Assets | £ |
|---|---|---|---|
| J. B.—Own capital | 32,800 | House, cost | 40,000 |
| Building society loan | 25,000 | Furniture, cost | 10,000 |
| Furniture shop | 700 | Car, cost | 8,000 |
|  |  | Cash at bank | 500 |
|  | £58,500 |  | £58,500 |

Figure 1

We can summarize J. B.'s balance sheet by saying that it is a statement containing two lists: assets and sources of finance. The list of assets has been drawn up in response to the question: "What valuable things do I own and how much did they cost?" The list of sources of finance has been drawn up in response to the question: "Who is financing these assets, and by how much?" Both sides add up to the same total, because a balance sheet looks at the same picture from two different angles: the sources from which finance is being obtained, and the form in which it is being held (the assets). A balance sheet is an expression of the fact that every asset has to be financed by someone.

## Classifying the Assets

It is helpful in the subsequent analysis of a balance sheet to subdivide the assets into different categories. An important distinction which is made by accountants when drawing up the assets side of a balance sheet is the distinction between fixed assets and current assets. Fixed assets are generally those assets with a relatively long life, which are held to be kept and used. In the balance sheet at Figure 2, J. B. has classified his house, furniture and car as fixed assets, indicating a primary intention of keeping and using these items. The primary intention in owning the house, for example, is to live in it rather than to sell it again.

J. B.'s account at the bank, however, is not held in order to be used

**J. B.**
**BALANCE SHEET**
*1st January*

| CAPITAL | £ | FIXED ASSETS | £ |
|---|---|---|---|
| J. B. | 32,800 | House, cost | 40,000 |
| LONG-TERM LIABILITY | | Furniture, cost | 10,000 |
| Building society loan | 25,000 | Car, cost | 8,000 |
| | | | 58,000 |
| CURRENT LIABILITY | | CURRENT ASSET | |
| Furniture shop | 700 | Cash at bank | 500 |
| | £58,500 | | £58,500 |

**Figure 2**

in its present form. It has been classified as a current asset, because it is primarily held for the purpose of meeting current expenditure, including paying bills and buying other assets. Similarly, if J. B. also had an asset such as an I.O.U. from a friend, which was to be converted into cash in the near future (say within the coming year), the amount owing would also be classified as a current asset.

In summary, we may say that fixed assets are generally those items which have a relatively long life and are acquired to be kept and used; whereas current assets generally consist of cash and items which are acquired with the intention of converting them into cash in the near future (usually within one year).

### Classifying the Sources of Finance

We have already noted that J. B. has two outside sources of finance on 1st January (the building society and the furniture shop), and that the remaining cost of his assets is being financed out of his own capital. The distinction between finance provided by the building society and the furniture shop, on the one hand, and J. B.'s own capital, on the other, is an important one. J. B.'s capital is, by definition, his own; whereas the finance provided by the two outside sources has to be paid off. This is the first classification which accountants make on the finance side of the balance sheet: the separation of capital, on the one hand, from loans and items which have to be paid off to outsiders, on the other. These latter items are classified as liabilities.

A further classification of liabilities is also made, and this is shown in the balance sheet at Figure 2. This is the distinction between long-term and current liabilities. Generally speaking, long-term liabilities are those items which have to be paid off twelve months or more from the date of the balance sheet; current liabilities are those which have to be paid within twelve months. In J. B.'s balance sheet at Figure 2, the building society loan has been classified as a long-term liability, indicating that it has more than one year to run; whereas the furniture shop account has probably only a month or two to run before it must be paid, and is therefore a current liability. (Strictly speaking, of course, J. B. should also classify as a current liability any payments to the building society which will fall due during the next twelve months, leaving only the remainder of the loan to be shown as a long-term liability.)

*The General Framework*

The general framework of a balance sheet may be summarized as follows:

BALANCE SHEET
(*At a certain date*)

| SOURCES OF FINANCE | ASSETS |
|---|---|
| CAPITAL | FIXED ASSETS<br>(To be kept and used) |
| LONG–TERM LIABILITIES<br>(Payable twelve months<br>or more hence) | |
| CURRENT LIABILITIES<br>(Payable within twelve<br>months) | CURRENT ASSETS<br>(Cash and items for conversion<br>into cash) |

Figure 3

*Recording Changes to Capital*

It is evident that a balance sheet, once prepared, is unlikely to remain up to date for long. It is a snapshot picture of a scene which is continually changing, and successive balance sheets will therefore be required, at intervals, showing the latest position and incorporating any changes which have taken place meanwhile.

Some changes which can occur in a balance sheet are relatively easy to appreciate. Changes will occur, for example, which affect only the assets side, e.g. more furniture may be bought for cash. This is a straightforward transaction to record, which would be reflected in a subsequent balance sheet by a reduction in the cash at bank, when the additional furniture is paid for, and a corresponding increase in the furniture. Other changes might affect both the assets and the liabilities, e.g. a current liability, such as the furniture-shop account, might be paid. In this case, a subsequent balance sheet would show a smaller bank balance, and the liability to the furniture shop would disappear.

More complicated changes occur, however, when something happens to alter the figure of capital in a balance sheet, and it is important to consider some of the more commonly found reasons why the figure of capital might change.

In the balance sheet at Figure 2 we noted that J. B.'s own capital was financing part of his assets to the extent of £32,800, the remaining £25,700 being financed by the building society and the furniture shop taken together. We also noted that the balance sheet was an expression of the fact that every asset has to be financed by someone, and we can express this by saying that finance represented by capital plus liabilities (long-term and current) must equal total assets (fixed and current). In J. B.'s balance sheet at Figure 2:

|  | £ |
|---|---|
| CAPITAL | 32,800 |
| + LIABILITIES | 25,700 |
| = ASSETS | £58,500 |

We can turn the equation round and say:

|  | £ |
|---|---|
| ASSETS | 58,500 |
| — LIABILITIES | 25,700 |
| = CAPITAL | £32,800 |

It is evident from this equation that one important factor which will affect the figure of capital shown in a balance sheet will be a change in the assets, without a corresponding change in the liabilities.

Three changes in assets which do not affect the liabilities, but which do affect the figure of capital, are of particular importance:

1. Assets may be revalued. In times of inflation a revaluation will cause an increase in the assets and an increase in the figure of capital.

2. Fixed assets may be depreciated, to allow for wear and tear and obsolescence. This will cause a fall in the assets and a corresponding fall in the figure of capital.

3. Part of income may be saved, so increasing the assets and increasing the figure of capital.

We can illustrate these changes to capital as they might affect J. B.'s balance sheet, and in so doing we will follow the terminology commonly found in limited companies' balance sheets, where the word 'Reserve' is used.

### Reserve—Revaluation of Assets

Suppose that, having drawn up his balance sheet as in Figure 2, J. B. decides to revalue his house. Inflation has occurred since J. B. first acquired the house and he feels that original cost is no longer an acceptable basis for valuing this asset. A valuation made on 1st February produces a figure of £50,000: an increase of £10,000 over original cost. The figure of assets in J. B.'s balance sheet will now rise by £10,000, his liabilities will remain the same (evidently he does not owe any more or less because a revaluation has taken place), and his capital will therefore be shown at a higher figure, as follows:

|  | £ |  |
|---|---|---|
| ASSETS | 68,500 | (£58,500 + £10,000) |
| − LIABILITIES | 25,700 |  |
| = CAPITAL | £42,800 |  |

These changes have been made in the new balance sheet at Figure 4, which we assume J. B. prepares one month later, on 1st February, assuming that no other transactions take place during the month.

J. B.
BALANCE SHEET
*1st February*

| CAPITAL | £ | FIXED ASSETS | £ |
|---|---|---|---|
| *1st January* | 32,800 | House, valuation | 50,000 |
| Reserve |  | Furniture, cost | 10,000 |
| Due to revaluation |  | Car, cost | 8,000 |
| of house | 10,000 |  |  |
| *Total* | 42,800 |  | 68,000 |
| LONG-TERM LIABILITY |  |  |  |
| Building society loan | 25,000 |  |  |
| CURRENT LIABILITY |  | CURRENT ASSET |  |
| Furniture shop | 700 | Cash at bank | 500 |
|  | £68,500 |  | £68,500 |

Figure 4

In drawing up his balance sheet at 1st February, J. B. has adopted the terminology frequently found in limited companies' balance sheets and has used the word reserve to describe the increase in the figure of capital following his decision to revalue the house.

It is at once evident that the word reserve, when shown on a balance sheet, has a different meaning from the popular usage of the word. A reserve in popular speech implies that a sum of money has been set aside. In popular speech the word reserve is therefore closely associated with cash. In accounting, the word reserve does not necessarily have anything to do with cash at all; and in this particular illustration the reserve now appearing for the first time on the balance sheet has nothing whatever to do with cash, which remains exactly the same as before, at £500.

A reserve, in the technical sense used by accountants, means that the figure of capital has increased; and in J. B.'s case the increase has been shown with an explanation—"due to revaluation of house". When reading a balance sheet, therefore, the word reserve should be interpreted in the technical sense, as meaning an increase in the figure of capital, and it should not be assumed that the creation of a reserve has necessarily altered the figure of cash at the bank.

*Depreciation*

A second reason why a change can take place in J. B.'s capital will occur if he decides to recognize the fact that some of his assets are wearing out or becoming obsolete. He may therefore decide to make an allowance for depreciation.

Suppose that he decides to deduct £100 in respect of depreciation on the car for the month of January. J. B.'s balance sheet at 1st February will now reflect this depreciation, which will reduce his assets by £100, leave his liabilities to the building society and the furniture shop unaltered, and therefore reduce his figure of capital as follows:

|  | £ |  |
|---|---|---|
| ASSETS | 68,400 | (£68,500 – £100) |
| – LIABILITIES | 25,700 | |
| = CAPITAL | £42,700 | |

The balance sheet at 1st February will now read as follows:

J. B.
BALANCE SHEET
*1st February*

| | | | Valuation or cost | Deprec-iation | Net |
|---|---|---|---|---|---|
| CAPITAL | £ | FIXED ASSETS | £ | £ | £ |
| 1st January | 32,800 | House, valuation | 50,000 | — | 50,000 |
| Reserve | | Furniture, cost | 10,000 | — | 10,000 |
| Due to revaluation | | Car, cost | 8,000 | 100 | 7,900 |
| of house | 10,000 | | | | |
| | | | £68,000 | £100 £67,900 | |
| *Decrease* | | | | | |
| Due to depreciation | | | | | |
| of car | (100) | | | | |
| *Total* | 42,700 | | | | |
| LONG-TERM LIABILITY | | | | | |
| Building society loan | 25,000 | | | | |
| CURRENT LIABILITY | | CURRENT ASSET | | | |
| Furniture shop | 700 | Cash at bank | | | 500 |
| | £68,400 | | | | £68,400 |

Figure 5

In this case, there has been a decrease in the figure of capital, due to the fact that a deduction has been made for depreciation. Again, no change occurs in J. B.'s bank account, which remains at £500, assuming that no other transactions take place during the month.

*Reserve—Savings*

A third change which can affect the figure of capital shown in the balance sheet will arise as J. B. earns income, e.g. earns a salary; and incurs expenses such as housekeeping and petrol. To the extent that his income after tax exceeds his expenses, he will have increased his capital by saving; to the extent that his expenses exceed his income after tax, he will have lived off his capital and so reduced it.

Suppose, for example, that J. B. earns £1,400 gross in salary during January, and that tax and expenses amount to £1,200, all expenses being paid for during the month, so that he saves £200. We will assume also that J. B. keeps this amount of savings in his bank account. J. B.'s assets will now rise by £200, his liabilities will remain the same, assuming no other transactions take place, and his figure of capital will rise as follows:

| | | |
|---|---|---|
| ASSETS | 68,600 | (£68,400 + £200) |
| − LIABILITIES | 25,700 | |
| = CAPITAL | £42,900 | |

J. B.'s balance sheet at 1st February (Figure 6) will show this increase in assets, and will also record the increase in capital. Again, the increase in capital is shown as a reserve, and in this particular case, because J. B. has decided to keep his savings in the bank, there *is* a corresponding rise in the bank account figure.

This need not be the case for very long, however, since J. B. may later decide to hold part of his savings in the form of an investment, which will yield him interest. In this case, when he invests his money, the bank account will be reduced, and a new item, 'Investment', will appear on the assets side of the balance sheet, so that once again a relationship need not necessarily exist between a reserve appearing in the balance sheet and the cash-at-bank figure. Of course, if J. B. decides to alter the form in which he holds his savings in this way, this does not alter the fact that the savings still exist. The £200 addition to capital under the heading of reserves therefore remains.

Alternatively, J. B. may later decide to draw out his savings. For example, he may decide to have a holiday using the £200, after which his savings would disappear from the balance sheet and his bank account would be reduced by £200.

It is evident, however, that J. B. would be imprudent if he spent the whole of his savings in this way without retaining something towards the eventual replacement of the car when it wears out.* In the balance sheet at Figure 6, the figure of £200 savings has been reduced by the £100 depreciation figure to produce a net amount of £100. This indicates to J. B. the maximum amount of savings he can draw out, if he is to retain an amount equal to the depreciation allowance on the car.

* J. B.'s furniture and house are also gradually wearing out or going obsolete, but for the sake of simplicity only the car is being considered.

J. B.
BALANCE SHEET
*1st February*

| CAPITAL | £ | £ | FIXED ASSETS | Valuation or cost £ | Depreci- ation £ | Net £ |
|---|---|---|---|---|---|---|
| *1st January* | | 32,800 | House, valuation | 50,000 | — | 50,000 |
| *Reserves* | | | Furniture, cost | 10,000 | — | 10,000 |
| Due to revaluation | | | Car, cost | 8,000 | 100 | 7,900 |
| of house | | 10,000 | | | | |
| | | | | £68,000 | £100 | £67,900 |
| Due to savings | 200 | | | | | |
| *Less* depreciation | 100 | 100 | | | | |
| *Total* | | 42,900 | | | | |
| LONG-TERM LIABILITY | | | | | | |
| Building society loan | | 25,000 | | | | |
| CURRENT LIABILITY | | | CURRENT ASSET | | | |
| Furniture shop | | 700 | Cash at bank | | | 700 |
| | | £68,600 | | | | £68,600 |

Figure 6

*Limited Company Balance Sheets—Assets*

We are now in a position to apply the framework and terms which we have used for J. B. to the financial position of a limited company.

In a limited company's balance sheet such as the one at Figure 7, the fixed assets will include such items as land and buildings, fixtures and fittings, and motor vehicles which are owned and used by the company. The company is not in business to buy and sell the assets, but to keep them and use them. Fixed assets will be shown at valuation or cost, less the cumulative depreciation on these assets to date.

Current assets will include stocks (shown either at cost or at market value, whichever is the lower), debtors (representing the value of customers' accounts outstanding at the balance sheet date, less an allowance for bad and doubtful accounts), and cash (in hand and at the bank). These assets consist of cash and items which are to be turned into cash as part of the activities of the business: cash will be used, among other things, to buy stocks; stocks will eventually be sold to customers, who become the company's debtors; and it is anticipated that the debtors' figure will eventually be converted into cash on settlement of the accounts. Some cash will be used to buy more stocks and the cycle of conversion will repeat continually. Meanwhile, the fixed assets are used as the means whereby this process of conversion may be carried out.

*Limited Company Balance Sheets—Share Capital and Reserves*

On the finance side of a limited company's balance sheet, the company will have obtained finance from its shareholders in the form of share capital. The share capital is shown separately from increases to it, which are shown as reserves. Two increases are shown in Figure 7: increase due to revaluation of land and buildings, and increase due to cumulative retained profits recorded in the company's profit and loss account. The total of share capital and reserves represents the shareholders' capital employed in the business.

As additional profits are earned during each period, they will be recorded in a profit and loss account for that period. Part of this profit is usually retained in the business and added to the cumulative amount retained to date on the profit and loss account, to produce a new cumulative figure. In similar fashion to J. B., each period's profits are calculated after allowing for depreciation, with the result that the company is retaining funds equal to the depreciation allowance, period by period.

Of course, the reserves in the balance sheet are not necessarily represented by a figure of cash; and sound management will ensure that any surplus cash is put to productive use, e.g. by buying more fixed assets, stocks etc.

*Limited Company Balance Sheets—Long-Term and Current Liabilities*

Long-term liabilities may appear on a limited company's balance sheet, if the company has borrowed on terms which include repayment twelve months or more after the balance-sheet date. These long-term liabilities are frequently known as debentures. They are often secured, e.g. by a mortgage, and are thus similar in nature to the building society loan appearing on J. B.'s balance sheet, although they need not necessarily be repayable by instalments. They may be repayable at some future date in a lump sum. In the illustration at Figure 7, the mortgage debentures are repayable some time between 1990 and 1995;

XYZ LIMITED
BALANCE SHEET
*1st February 1979*

| | | | Valuation or Cost | Depreci- ation | Net |
|---|---|---|---|---|---|
| SHARE CAPITAL | £'000 | FIXED ASSETS | £'000 | £'000 | £'000 |
| 10 m. £1 Ordinary shares, fully paid | 10,000 | Land and buildings, at valuation | 13,500 | 1,500 | 12,000 |
| RESERVES | | Fixtures and fittings, | | | |
| Due to revaluation of land and buildings | 3,500 | at cost | 4,400 | 1,800 | 2,600 |
| Cumulative retained profit | 6,000 | Motor vehicles, at cost | 2,000 | 600 | 1,400 |
| SHAREHOLDERS' CAPITAL EMPLOYED | 19,500 | | 19,900 | 3,900 | 16,000 |

| | | | | | |
|---|---|---|---|---|---|
| LONG-TERM LIABILITIES | | | | | |
| 8% Mortgage Debentures 1990/95 | 2,000 | | | | |

| CURRENT LIABILITIES | | | CURRENT ASSETS | | |
|---|---|---|---|---|---|
| | £'000 | | | £'000 | |
| Creditors | 3,000 | | Stocks (at lower of cost or market value) | 5,000 | |
| Dividends payable | 500 | | Debtors | 3,000 | |
| Tax | 1,000 | 4,500 | Cash | 2,000 | 10,000 |
| | | 26,000 | | | 26,000 |

Figure 7

meanwhile the company has to pay 8% interest to the debenture holders.

Current liabilities in the balance sheet of a limited company will usually consist of items which have to be paid off within twelve months of the balance-sheet date, including such items as creditors, representing suppliers' accounts outstanding (similar to the furniture shop account in J. B.'s balance sheet), dividends declared but not paid at the date of the balance sheet, and the current tax liability.

*Alternative Balance Sheet Layouts*

Several alternative layouts to the one illustrated in Figure 7 are found in practice. For example, continental European balance sheets may have the assets listed on the left-hand side and the finance on the right. American balance sheets may also adopt this layout and, in addition, list the items in inverse order so that, for example, the list of assets in Figure 7 would start with cash and end with land and buildings.

One form of balance sheet which is worth highlighting in particular is a vertical presentation in summary form, in which the longer term investment and finance in a business is highlighted. Using only the totals in Figure 7, the balance sheet would appear as in Figure 8.

|  | £'000 | £'000 |
|---|---|---|
| FIXED ASSETS |  | 16,000 |
| CURRENT ASSETS | 10,000 |  |
| − CURRENT LIABILITIES | 4,500 |  |
| WORKING CAPITAL |  | 5,500 |
|  |  | 21,500 |
| SHAREHOLDERS' CAPITAL |  |  |
| EMPLOYED |  | 19,500 |
| LONG-TERM LIABILITIES |  | 2,000 |
|  |  | 21,500 |

Figure 8

(Footnotes to the balance sheet would provide the details as to the make-up of the individual headings.)

Notice that in this form of presentation the current liabilities are deducted from the current assets to show the working capital of the business: the amount of the longer-term capital which is needed to finance the excess of the current assets over the current liabilities.

*Ratio Analysis*

Many ratios and comparisons may be made involving figures appearing in a balance sheet, and as with accounting generally, specific purposes require specific ratios.

Two sets of ratios are of particular interest to managers, however: those related to profitability (where balance sheet figures are used in conjunction with figures taken from a profit and loss account for a particular period); and those related to liquidity, i.e. to the ability of a company to pay its short-term debts. These ratios are of interest because they can lead managers to a better understanding of the strengths and weaknesses of a business and of individual sections of it, and can lead to more effective managerial planning and control.

*Ratios related to Profitability*

Ratios related to profitability are concerned with the amount of profit earned during a period of time in relation to the capital employed in a business. Before discussing these ratios, however, it should be noted that capital employed is a term which is capable of a variety of definitions. For example, some companies equate capital employed with the shareholders' capital employed, i.e. with share capital and reserves. Others include long-term liabilities as well, as a semi-permanent source of finance. In the balance sheet at Figure 8, for example, the former view would regard capital employed as £19,500,000, while the latter would regard it as £21,500,000.

For the purposes of management accounting, there is something to be said for not making such distinctions between various sources of finance, but relating a figure of profit to a figure of *total assets*. Figure 7, for example, showed £26,000,000 as the total assets. This total assets approach is based on the view that the management of a company has a responsibility for all the resources owned by the company; and whether financed by shareholders' capital employed, by long term liabilities, or by incurring current liabilities, management should ensure that these resources earn an adequate return.

A number of adjustments are sometimes found to be necessary before a profitability ratio may be calculated. For example, it may be considered necessary to revalue some assets before making profitability comparisons between companies belonging to the same group, where such companies acquired their assets on different dates and are valuing them at different price levels. The profit figure may also be re-calculated to show operating profit before deducting loan interest and tax. These and similar adjustments will be made by the accountant in calculating the ratios.

For the purposes of illustration, profitability will be expressed simply in terms of the ratio profit/total assets. From this ratio a series of other ratios may be calculated, each dealing with a particular aspect of business affecting profitability. One of these will be the profit/sales ratio (the profit margin) and another will be the sales/total assets ratio (total asset turnover).

These two ratios taken together equal the profitability ratio, as shown in Figure 9 below. ("Sales" cancels out when the two ratios are multiplied together.)

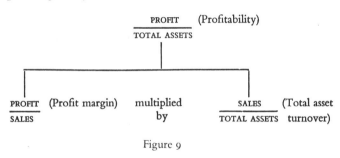

Figure 9

It is evident from Figure 9 that an acceptable rate of profit on total assets can be achieved by various combinations of profit margin and total asset turnover. For example, certain types of retail businesses, such as cut-price stores, operate on low profit margins, but carry fast-moving stocks, and in some cases also carry a relatively low investment in fixed assets (such as in shop fittings and delivery vehicles) in relation to their sales. These businesses therefore operate on a low profit/sales ratio in combination with a high sales/total assets ratio to produce an acceptable rate of profit on total assets.

On the other hand, some businesses might have a low total asset turnover and a high profit margin. An example might be a spare-parts manufacturer, who may require to own relatively expensive equipment and will probably carry stocks of slow-moving parts, following a policy of being able to satisfy customer demand whenever possible. Such a business would compensate for a low sales/total assets ratio by a high profit/sales ratio, to produce an acceptable rate of profit on total assets.

Each of the two ratios, profit/sales and sales/total assets, may be further broken down. An example of such a breakdown is given in Figure 10.

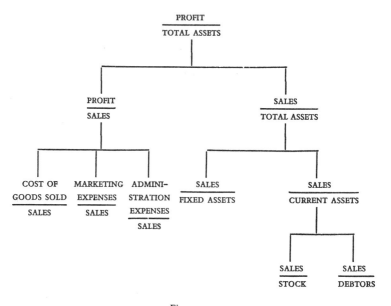

Figure 10

The profit/sales ratio will be affected by the costs and expenses incurred in earning the profit: the cost of goods sold and the expenses of the various departments will each, as it were, take a bite out of every pound of sales, so that the more that goes in costs and expenses the less is left for profit. Figure 10 illustrates three items particularly affecting the profit/sales ratio: cost of goods sold, marketing expenses and administration expenses. These items are each expressed as a ratio of sales, or they could be expressed as a percentage of sales (another form of ratio), to give an indication of the proportion of sales income absorbed by each. Further departmental or expense breakdowns could of course be provided, to suit particular businesses or particular circumstances.

On the assets side of Figure 10, since total assets comprise both fixed and current, the sales/total assets ratio may be broken down into sales/fixed assets and sales/current assets, each indicating the amount of business generated in relation to the assets employed. Changes in the sales/fixed assets ratio could be used as an approximate indicator of capacity utilization: a measure of how hard the fixed assets are being worked. The sales/current assets ratio is perhaps more useful if broken down into its main constituents: sales/stock and sales/debtors.

The sales/stock ratio is an approximate indicator of the rate of turnover of stock: an approximate guide to the speed with which stock moves through the business.* The sales/debtors ratio is an indicator of the speed with which customers settle their accounts on average, so that, for example, if annual credit sales were £1,200, and customers' accounts outstanding were on average £200, the sales/debtors ratio would be 1200/200, or six times a year. A turnover of six times a year would indicate that customers were taking, on average, two months before they paid their accounts.

These various ratios can be used to watch trends over a period of time; and, provided the various figures have been calculated on comparable bases, can also be used to make comparisons between similar businesses. Comparisons may be made between budget and actual ratios, and in some cases it may also be possible to compare a ratio with an independent standard, such as in the case of the sales/debtors ratio, where the period of credit granted to customers by the company's own terms of trade establishes a standard against which to compare the average period of credit which customers are in fact taking.

These ratios are, of course, using figures of assets with figures taken from a profit and loss account for a period: sales, cost of goods sold, expenses and profit. (The profit and loss account will be dealt with in more detail in Chapter 2.)

*Summary of Ratios related to Profitability*

We can summarize the ratios related to profitability which we have illustrated, as follows:

1. *Profit/Total Assets.* An overall indicator of the effectiveness of

---

* More accurate stock turnover ratios may be calculated, e.g. cost of goods sold/stock. Another stock turnover ratio, based on quantities, will be illustrated in Chapter 2.

the use made by management of the resources owned by the business.

2. *Sales/Total Assets*. Total asset turnover: the amount of business generated in relation to the total assets employed.

3. *Profit/Sales*. Profit margin: a measure of the average profit earned on sales.

4, 5 and 6. *Cost of Goods Sold, Marketing and Administration Expenses/Sales*. Indicators of the proportion of sales income absorbed by important items of costs and expenses.

7. *Sales/Fixed Assets*. An indicator of the volume of business generated with the use of the assets which are to be kept and used.

8. *Sales/Current Assets*. An indicator of the rate of turnover of assets which are in the process of conversion into cash.

9. *Sales/Stock*. An approximate indicator of the rate of turnover of stock, providing an approximate guide to the speed with which stock moves through business.

10. *Sales/Debtors*. An indicator of debtors' turnover, measuring the speed with which customers settle their accounts on average. This ratio can also be expressed in (say) months, to give a clearer picture of the average time customers are taking to pay.

*Ratios Related to Liquidity*

We saw earlier how the current assets are in a continuous state of conversion from stock to debtors to cash. Various managers have their part to play in the process. For example, in the case of a manufacturing company, the buyer, by placing an order, eventually causes cash to be converted into a stock of raw materials; the production manager takes the stock of raw materials and converts it into a stock of finished goods, carrying at any one point in time a stock of work in progress, representing semi-finished goods in the factory. The marketing manager sells and distributes the finished goods to customers, who become the company's debtors. The accountant ensures that the customers' accounts are recorded and eventually settled in cash. Part of the cash is used to buy more raw materials and the cycle of conversion repeats. At the same time, current liabilities are created, and later settled in cash, not the least of which will be accounts of suppliers who have provided the business with goods and services on credit.

The balance sheet has of course frozen this activity to present a picture of the state of the current assets and current liabilities at a moment of time. For example, a manufacturing company's balance sheet would include many of the following headings:

| | £ | | £ |
|---|---|---|---|
| CURRENT LIABILITIES | | CURRENT ASSETS | |
| Creditors | xxx | Stock of raw materials | xxx |
| | | Stock of work in progress | xxx |
| | | Stock of finished goods | xxx |
| | | Debtors | xxx |
| | | Cash | xxx |

From the balance sheet two ratios may be prepared which particularly relate to the liquidity of the business: to its ability to meet its short-term debts.

*Current Assets : Current Liabilities (Current Ratio)*

A comparison between current assets and current liabilities will give an indication of the degree to which the company is able to pay its short-term debts. It is often considered prudent to allow a margin of current assets over current liabilities, and a frequently quoted ratio for a healthy financial state is that current assets should be approximately twice current liabilities, i.e. that the ratio should be about 2:1. The 2:1 yardstick should, however, be looked upon only as an average, which will inevitably vary from one business to another, and in seasonal businesses from one season to another. Some current assets are, of course, farther away than others from the stage of conversion into cash: stocks of raw materials in a manufacturing company, for example, are farthest away from being turned into cash; whereas debtors are only one stage removed from cash, so that evidently the proportion of the various items in the current asset total also has a bearing on the interpretation of this ratio.

A useful practice is to watch movements in the ratio over a period of time, with the object of seeing whether the ability of the company to meet its short-term debts appears to be improving or worsening. It should be noted that a very high ratio, although strong from a liquidity point of view, may not be so desirable from a profitability point of view, since there may be surplus current assets, e.g. surplus cash on hand, earning a nil or an inadequate rate of return.

*Cash\* and Debtors : Current Liabilities (Acid-Test Ratio)*

This comparison is a more stringent test of a company's ability to pay its short-term debts. Stocks are left out of the comparison as being the farthest away from cash, and so the comparison is between the total of ready money and near-ready money, and the current liabilities. An often quoted standard for this comparison is that a healthy financial state exists when cash and debtors are approximately equal to current liabilities, i.e. a 1:1 ratio. Again, a ratio of 1:1 is not an absolute standard but will vary from one business to another.

It is also useful to review trends in this ratio over a period of time, and this is particularly the case when a business is expanding. Companies which are expanding rapidly can sometimes find themselves embarrassed by a lack of ready money to pay their current liabilities. For example, a company may increase its stock levels during an expansion phase, by buying stock on credit from suppliers. If the company continues to do this it may eventually be embarrassed by a lack of ready money, simply because its creditors may require payment long before the stock has been converted into cash. A regular review of the proportion of cash and debtors to current liabilities will help to avoid this situation.

It is evident from the above that two of the ratios related to profitability are also related to liquidity: sales/stock, providing an approximate guide to the speed with which stock moves through the business; and sales/debtors, measuring the speed with which customers settle their accounts on average. These two ratios give an indication of the speed with which stock and debtors are moving towards cash.

It is also possible to indicate the speed with which cash moves in the other direction, towards creditors, by calculating the average period of credit which a company is taking before paying its suppliers. This is commonly measured by the ratio purchases/creditors, so that if annual purchases were £960 and suppliers' accounts outstanding were on average £120, the purchases/creditors ratio would be 960/120 or 8 times a year. A turnover of 8 times a year would indicate that the company was taking 12/8, or $1\frac{1}{2}$, months' credit, on average, before paying its suppliers' accounts. Regular review of these turnover ratios, therefore, also helps to maintain a healthy financial position.

\* Cash for this purpose also includes such items as short-term investments which could be turned into cash at relatively short notice.

*Some Dangers and Limitations*

It is important for managers to remember the dangers and limitations of using balance sheets, and the type of ratios we have been considering, in the analysis of a business. Five dangers and limitations are of particular importance.

1. A balance sheet is a snapshot picture of the state of a business at a moment in time, although in reality the picture will be continually changing. The balance sheet may not, therefore, always be representative of the average position. This is a particular possibility in businesses affected by the seasons, where the assets and liabilities can be significantly different, according to whether the balance sheet has been drawn up at the high or low season date.

2. Inflation has caused asset values to change, and these changes may or may not be reflected in the balance sheet. Because there is a possibility that assets may have been acquired or valued on different dates at different price levels, comparisons between one set of figures and another in times of inflation *might*, therefore, be misleading unless the figures are first adjusted.

3. Even when price levels are constant, accounting figures may be calculated differently, as there is often more than one method of accounting which could be adopted. This particularly affects the fixed assets and stock figures, and the calculation of profit, as we will see in more detail in Chapter 4. However, the existence of different methods of calculation is usually much less of a problem when comparing figures for one company over a period of time, or when making budget/actual comparisons, or when comparing the figures of companies within the same group, because in all these cases it is likely that the accountants concerned will be consistent in the methods they adopt, or will indicate where significant changes in method have occurred. Comparisons between figures for completely unrelated companies, however, *might* be subject to error because of the possibility that different methods of calculation have been adopted.

4. Even if limitations 1 to 3 did not exist, any accounting statement could never present a complete picture of a business; and a balance sheet is no exception to this. Accounting is basically concerned with things that can be measured in money terms, and this obviously leaves out of account qualitative considerations, which

may be of great importance to managers in the assessment of a business situation, e.g. staff morale and the quality of personnel. These factors of course eventually influence the financial results, but they cannot be represented, as such, in figure form.

5. With particular regard to ratio analysis, managers should not feel that it will provide an easy road to the solution of business problems. Such analysis should be looked upon more as a logical way of beginning an assessment of a business situation, which should enable the manager to focus his attention on some (but not necessarily all) of its essential features, and stimulate him to ask further pertinent questions. For example, ratio analysis might indicate that a trend towards lower profitability was due to a worsening sales/debtors ratio. But this in turn might be caused by bad credit control at the stage of opening new customers' accounts; failure to invoice promptly; failure to send out statements promptly; failure to review overdue accounts periodically; failure to send out reminders to customers who are late in payment; shortage of staff in the invoicing or accounting sections; or simply by a general softening of trade in which customers are taking longer to pay because they are short of cash. The sales/debtors ratio will not pinpoint which of these particular factors is at work in the situation, but it has guided the manager to a selected area of the business which appears to need attention. Only after further investigation, however, including an assessment of the human factors in the situation, will the manager be in a position to decide what action, if any, is needed.

### Summary

This outline of accounting techniques which are particularly relevant to a manager in the analysis of a business began with the balance sheet. We saw how the balance sheet was basically made up of two lists, assets and sources of finance; and how the assets were classified into fixed and current, and the sources of finance into capital, reserves, long-term liabilities and current liabilities.

We saw how a business could be analysed by ratio analysis. Various ratios particularly related to profitability were outlined, together with further ratios related to liquidity, and some inter-relationships between the ratios noted.

Finally, some of the more important dangers and limitations in using balance sheets and ratio analysis were considered.

# 2 PLANNING FOR OPERATIONS

The previous chapter explained how the accountant summarizes certain salient facts about a business in the form of a balance sheet. The balance sheet was seen to be a financial snapshot, recording the position of a business as it existed at one point in time. We noted that the picture is, however, continually changing as business activity takes place, and so the balance sheet is perhaps more appropriately looked upon as one frame out of a cine film continuously recording the activity of a business.

Our objective in this chapter is to trace the steps necessary to move from one frame in the film to a subsequent frame, i.e. from a balance sheet at the beginning of a budget period, to a budgeted balance sheet at the end: the link between the two being provided by a set of budget accounts.

*Advantages of Preparing Budget Accounts*

The preparation of a set of budget accounts has a number of advantages. It is a way of focusing managers' attention consciously and systematically on the future, particularly on likely developments in the environment in which a business operates; and on possible developments within the business itself. Managers are required to express their intentions for the future in numerical form, and this is likely to encourage a greater degree of clear thinking and precision than might otherwise be the case.

By expressing budgets in financial terms, by converting quantities into the common denominator of money, an additional dimension is introduced. The use of money as a common unit of measurement enables the plans of the individual members of the management team to be related to each other and summarized together. The greater possibility now exists of integrating the plans of individual managers in the various departments of the business, and of reconciling, in advance, the sometimes conflicting requirements of different departments. This integration of the planned activities of the members of the management team is a significant advantage arising out of the preparation of a set of budget accounts, as a consequence of which each member of the team has an agreed role to play in the achievement of a common objective.

The use of the money measure also enables the financial implications of budget proposals to be foreseen, and provision made for the necessary cash resources to be made available as required. The financial soundness and profitability of the proposals can also be judged in advance, by the use of ratios and other comparisons.

Finally, budget accounts and their supporting schedules provide a basis for comparison with actual performance, enabling individual managers to see where performance deviates from plan and where corrective action is required. Delegation of responsibility for the achievement of plan, and of authority for taking corrective action, are thereby facilitated.

The preparation of a set of budget accounts may be summed up as an exercise involving both managers and accountants, requiring anticipated future events to be expressed in quantitative and money terms, integrated into a company plan and assessed from a financial viewpoint.

### The Budget Period

The period of time we will adopt for the purpose of illustrating a set of budget accounts will be three months, from 1st January to 31st March. This is not, of course, meant to imply that companies necessarily adopt this period of time in practice.

Many companies adopt the practice of preparing annual budgets for operations, phased at monthly or quarterly intervals, together with a longer-term budget, possibly extending over five years or more, for expenditure on fixed assets such as the erection of new buildings.

The set of budget accounts illustrated in this chapter may therefore be looked upon as the first phase of a longer look into the future.

### Budget Accounts Illustrated

In the first part of this chapter we will be tracing through the steps needed to build up a balance sheet at the close of a budget period. Readers will find it helpful to prepare their own budgeted balance sheets separately as they read through the chapter, so they are recommended to write out at this stage the headings found in Figure 28, page 44, (excluding the figures, and items in brackets) and fill in the figures for themselves as they go. Guidance for the completion of the budgeted balance sheet will be found in brackets at appropriate intervals throughout the chapter. Figure 28 will provide a check on readers' figures at the end.

The examples in this chapter will be kept simple so that the essentials of budget accounts may be understood. The general framework of a set of budget accounts will be dealt with first, using as an illustration a set of figures related to a non-manufacturing organization, followed by an outline of the additional budgets which a manufacturing organization generally requires.

## Opening Balance Sheet 1st January

In our illustration we begin with an opening balance sheet at 1st January (Figure 11). This opening balance sheet will itself be an estimate of the position at 1st January rather than a statement of the actual position, simply because the preparation of budgets will begin some time before the budget period starts.

OPENING BALANCE SHEET
*1st January*

|  | £'000 |  | *Valuation or Cost* £'000 | *Depreciation* £'000 | *Net* £'000 |
|---|---|---|---|---|---|
| SHARE CAPITAL | 400 | FIXED ASSETS | 315 | 80 | 235 |
| RESERVES |  |  |  |  |  |
| Cumulative retained profit | 260 |  |  |  |  |
|  | — |  |  |  |  |
| SHAREHOLDERS' CAPITAL EMPLOYED | 660 |  |  |  |  |
| CURRENT LIABILITIES | | CURRENT ASSETS |  |  |  |
| £'000 | | | £'000 |  |  |
| Creditors 260 | | Stock, at cost | 375 |  |  |
| | | Debtors | 300 |  |  |
| Tax 90 | | Cash | 100 |  |  |
| — | 350 | — |  |  | 775 |
|  | 1,010 |  |  |  | 1,010 |

Figure 11

A preliminary assessment of the financial position of the company may be made by considering the two ratios particularly related to liquidity, which were outlined in the previous chapter. After a set of budget accounts has been prepared we will again refer to these ratios,

and compare them with those relating to the balance sheet at the end
of the budget period to observe the trend.

*Current Assets: Current Liabilities (Current Ratio)*. The ratio is 775/350,
or 2·2:1.

*Cash and Debtors : Current Liabilities (Acid Test Ratio)*. The ratio is
400/350, or 1·1:1.

*Budgets to be Prepared*

In order to draw up a budgeted balance sheet showing the position
of the company at 31st March, it will be necessary to anticipate changes
which are likely to take place in the various balance sheet items during
the budget period.

These changes may be summarized by referring to the balance sheet
headings in Figure 11.

On the assets side, the management of the company will have to
consider what changes, if any, are likely to take place in:

    1. the investment in fixed assets: whether additional items are to
be acquired, or items disposed of;

    2. the investment in current assets: the stock holding, and whether
stocks will be built up or run down during the budget period; the
debtors figure, and whether the value of customers' accounts outstanding at 31st March is expected to show an increase or decrease on
the opening figure; the cash figure, and what movements of cash, in
and out, are likely to take place during the budget period.

On the finance side, consideration will have to be given to:

    3. any additional share capital which is proposed to be issued;

    4. likely changes in the figure of reserves: in particular, changes
due to the retention in the business of profits to be earned during the
budget period. This will require a careful assessment of:

    (a) the value of sales for the period;

    (b) the cost of the goods to be sold, and the expenses to be in-
curred in running the business;

    (c) the amount of the resultant profit to be appropriated for taxes
and dividends; and hence the cumulative amount to be
retained in the business at the end of the period's operations.

    5. changes during the budget period to the figure of creditors and
to the tax liability, and whether any other liabilities are to be incurred during the budget period.

## The Limiting Factor

The general scheme is therefore that budgets will be required of changes to the items listed 1 to 5 above.

The next problem to consider is the factor which will limit the scale of the company's operations during the budget period (known as the limiting factor). The scale of operations may be limited by a wide variety of factors in practice, but three of importance may be identified: sales, supplies and finance.

In most cases it is the ability of the company to penetrate the market which sets the upper limit to the scale of operations during the budget period. In other cases, however, the availability of supplies, e.g. of goods for resale, can set the upper limit. In still other cases the scale of operations may be restricted to a level which can be supported by available finance.

In our illustration of a set of budget accounts the most usual case will be assumed: that the limiting factor during the budget period will be the level of sales which can be achieved. The sales budget will therefore set the level of activity to which the other budgets will be geared.

## Sales Budget

Sales budget preparation is basically the responsibility of the marketing function in a company, aided by the accountant, who may be able to assist by providing such information as trend data of sales, analysed by products, product groups, salesmen, etc. In practice, sales budget preparation will require the preparation of a number of subsidiary schedules, generally showing quantities to be sold and budgeted selling prices, analysed by managerial responsibilities and by products or product groups.

For the purposes of illustration we will assume that the sales budget for the period 1st January—31st March relates to one product as in Figure 12.

SALES BUDGET
*1st January—31st March*

| Quantity Units | Selling Price £ | Value £ |
|---|---|---|
| 500,000 | 2·00 | 1,000,000 |

Figure 12

Later in the chapter we will discuss the preparation of a budget showing the expenses of running the marketing department. It is likely, however, that preliminary estimates of selling expenses will also be prepared at this stage, since the weight of selling effort will influence the preparation of the sales figures themselves.

*Stock Budget*

Closely related to the sales budget is the budget for stocks of goods to be sold to customers. The opening stock at 1st January is shown in the balance sheet at Figure 11 at £375,000, representing the cost of stock on hand at that date. Assuming that the cost price of this stock was £1·50 per unit, the opening stock figure can be summarized as shown in Figure 13.

OPENING STOCK
*1st January*

| Quantity Units | Cost Price £ | Cost £ |
|---|---|---|
| 250,000 | 1·50 | 375,000 |

Figure 13

A budget must now be prepared showing the closing stock position at 31st March. This budget will generally be the responsibility of the stock controller or stores manager, working in co-operation with the sales manager, the buyer and the accountant. The stock budget, in many cases, will be a compromise between the requirements of these various managers. The stock controller will perhaps be conscious of space limitations in the stores; the sales manager will wish to have ample supplies to meet his sales figures and maintain customer satisfaction by prompt deliveries; the buyer may prefer to buy in bulk and take advantage of quantity discounts; and the accountant will be conscious of the money locked up in stocks and the need to watch liquidity and profitability.

One simple approach with which to begin the preparation of a stock budget, would be to use stock turnover rates. The calculation could be based on a required stock turnover rate, expressed in terms of the number of weeks' sales which are to be kept in stock. Suppose that the policy initially set for the budget period is to maintain a quantity of 6½ weeks' sales in stock, i.e. one half of the coming quarter's sales are to be kept in stock. Since stock is held in anticipation of sales, in order to assess the quantity of stock at 31st March, it will be necessary to prepare a further sales budget figure for the quarter April—June.

Suppose that a sales budget for the quarter April—June shows sales of 640,000 units. If 6½ weeks' sales are to be kept in stock, the required stock holding at 31st March will be 320,000 units (640,000÷2). If the budgeted cost price of stock is fixed at £1·50 per unit, a stock budget at 31st March can now be prepared as follows:

STOCK BUDGET
*31st March*

| Quantity Units | Cost Price £ | Cost £ |
|---|---|---|
| 320,000 | 1·50 | 480,000 |

Figure 14

This type of calculation represents one of the simpler methods of preparing a stock budget, and, as noted above, the results may well be modified as part of a reconciliation of managers' interests. More sophisticated techniques, such as operational research formulae, may also be used to assist in the preparation of stock budgets. (Assuming, for illustration purposes, that the budget is agreed as at Figure 14, the cost of stock to be held on 31st March may now be entered by readers in their budgeted balance sheets.)

*Purchases Budget*

The figures established so far can be used to calculate the amount of purchases required, as shown in Figure 15.

| | Quantity Units | *Source* |
|---|---|---|
| Required for sales, Jan.—March | 500,000 | Sales budget (Figure 12) |
| Required for stock, 31st March | 320,000 | Stock budget (Figure 14) |
| Total required | 820,000 | |
| *Less* available from stock, 1st January | 250,000 | Figure 13 |
| Purchases required | 570,000 units | |

Figure 15

Valuing this figure of 570,000 units, to be purchased at a budgeted cost price of £1·50 per unit, produces a purchases budget as in Figure 16.

PURCHASES BUDGET
*1st Jan—31st March*

| Quantity Units | Cost Price £ | Cost £ |
|---|---|---|
| 570,000 | 1·50 | 855,000 |

Figure 16

*Profit and Loss Budget: Gross Profit*

It is now possible to summarize the monetary equivalents of the activity budgeted for so far, in the form of a profit and loss budget showing the gross profit.

PROFIT AND LOSS BUDGET
(showing Gross Profit)
*1st Jan.—31st March*

|  | £ | £ | Source |
|---|---|---|---|
| Sales budget |  | 1,000,000 | Figure 12 |
| Purchases budget | 855,000 |  | Figure 16 |
| Opening stock, 1st Jan: | 375,000 |  | Figure 13 |
| *Cost of goods to be available* | 1,230,000 |  |  |
| *Less* Stock budget, 31st March | 480,000 |  | Figure 14 |
| *Cost of goods to be sold* |  | 750,000 |  |
| Budgeted gross profit (25% on sales) |  | £  250,000 |  |

Figure 17

The inner column of the profit and loss budget shows the cost of purchases to be made during the budget period, to which is added the cost of stock on hand at 1st January, making the total cost of goods to be available. From this figure is deducted the cost of goods to be held in stock on 31st March, leaving the cost of goods to be sold during the budget period. In the outer column of the budget, the difference between the sales value of the goods to be sold and their cost is the budgeted gross profit.

In this illustration, the company is budgeting for a gross profit of 25% on sales, i.e. the cost of goods to be sold represents 75% of sales. In Chapter 1 (Figure 10) we saw that the ratio cost of goods sold/sales is one of the ratios influencing over-all profitability, so that the acceptability of this figure will be a matter for consideration by top management.

### Departmental Expenses Budgets

In order to arrive at a budgeted net profit, the expenses to be incurred in operating the various departments of the business will have to be budgeted for. We will assume for illustration purposes that there are only two departments to consider:

*Marketing:* including advertising, selling and distribution;

*Administration:* including buying, stock control, personnel, accounting and general management.

Detailed schedules of expenses will be required for each of these departments, built up by the individual managers concerned, working in co-operation with the accountant. The schedules will require details of the various types of expenses to be incurred, e.g. marketing department schedules might include details of:

Salaries
commissions
entertainment
car expenses
advertising.

The expenses will be scheduled according to the responsibilities of individual managers, so that the budgets can later be used for comparison with actual performance.

Where appropriate, the departmental expenses figures will be geared to the level of activity budgeted for; salesmen's commissions, for example, may be calculated in relation to the budgeted value of sales.

Summarized departmental expenses budgets will be required for incorporation in the profit and loss budget. The assumed figures for the purposes of illustration are as shown in Figure 18.

DEPARTMENTAL EXPENSES BUDGETS
*1st January—31st March*

| | £ | |
|---|---|---|
| Marketing | 50,000 | (including £5,000 depreciation on fixed assets used by the department). |
| Administration | 150,000 | (including £10,000 depreciation on fixed assets used by the department). |
| | £200,000 | |

Figure 18

(The £15,000 total depreciation expense for the budget period may now be added to the cumulative depreciation figure in the opening balance sheet (Figure 11) and a new cumulative figure entered in the budgeted balance sheet).

### Profit and Loss Budget: Net Profit

The departmental expenses budgets are deducted from the budgeted gross profit, as calculated at Figure 17, to arrive at the budgeted net profit, shown in Figure 19.

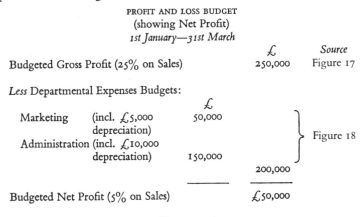

PROFIT AND LOSS BUDGET
(showing Net Profit)
*1st January—31st March*

|  | £ | | £ | Source |
|---|---|---|---|---|
| Budgeted Gross Profit (25% on Sales) | | | 250,000 | Figure 17 |
| *Less* Departmental Expenses Budgets: | | | | |
| Marketing (incl. £5,000 depreciation) | 50,000 | | | Figure 18 |
| Administration (incl. £10,000 depreciation) | 150,000 | | 200,000 | |
| Budgeted Net Profit (5% on Sales) | | | £50,000 | |

Figure 19

Figure 19 shows a budgeted net profit of 5% on sales. This figure will again be subject to scrutiny by top management, and if considered to be inadequate, reduction may have to be made in the marketing and administration expenses budgets.

Assuming, however, that the net profit at 5% on sales is accepted, we are in a position to complete the profit and loss budget, by calculating the amount of profit which will be appropriated for taxes and dividends, and the amount which will be retained in the business.

### Profit and Loss Budget: Taxes, Dividends and Retained Profit

Taxation calculations will be performed by the company's accountant or by the company's professional advisers, taking into account the various tax allowances which the company can claim. The amount of profit to be appropriated for dividends will be considered by top management and the accountant, taking into account such factors as the company's own needs for finance and the rate of dividend expected by the shareholders. We will assume that tax based on the profits for the period Jan.—March is estimated at £20,000; and that dividends will appropriate £10,000.

The profit and loss budget may therefore be completed as in Figure 20.

PROFIT AND LOSS BUDGET
(showing Taxes, Dividends and Retained Profit)
*1st January—31st March*

|  | £ | Source |
|---|---|---|
| Budgeted net profit (5% on Sales) | 50,000 | Figure 19 |
| less Tax | 20,000 | See para. above |
| Budgeted net profit after tax | 30,000 | |
| Cumulative retained profit at 1st January | 260,000 | Figure 11 |
|  | 290,000 | |
| less Dividends | 10,000 | See para. above |
| Cumulative retained profit at 31st March | £280,000 | |

Figure 20

The budgeted net profit after tax, £30,000, is added to the cumulative retained profit at 1st January, shown in the opening balance sheet at Figure 11. This produces a figure of £290,000 which is the maximum amount of dividend that may be declared. The proposed appropriation for dividends is only £10,000 however, leaving a proposed £280,000 cumulative retained profit at 31st March.

(In drawing up this profit and loss budget three additional figures

have been created which may now be entered by readers in their
budgeted balance sheets:

|  | £'000 |
|---|---|
| Cumulative Retained Profit | 280 |
| (Reserves) |  |
| Tax | 20 |
| (A current liability until paid) |  |
| Dividends | 10 |
| (A current liability until paid) |  |

## Summary

The preparation of the foregoing set of budgets began with the
opening balance sheet, followed by an assessment of the factors likely
to limit the scale of the company's operations during the budget period.

The preparation of a profit and loss budget required a number of
managers to submit details of their intended actions in quantities and
in money terms, in the form of a sales budget, a stock budget, a
purchases budget and departmental expenses budgets. In integrating
these various budgets a reconciliation of the interests of the various
managers concerned was required, including an assessment of the
figures by top management. Budgeted tax appropriation and dividend
appropriation figures were also prepared, leading to a new cumulative
figure of retained profit.

In this process, individual managers were directly involved in
creating budgets for their own spheres of responsibility, so that
budgets have been set for later comparison with actual performance.
A company profit plan has been created with individual managers
having a defined role to play in its achievement.

Further budgets must now be prepared which relate more closely
to the finance aspect of future operations.

## Debtors Budget

Attention must be given to the changes which are likely to take
place during the budget period in the figure of debtors, shown in the
opening balance sheet at £300,000 (Figure 11). The debtors budget
will be prepared by the accountant in conjunction with marketing
management. The budget will include the opening debtors figure, the
value of invoices to be rendered to customers, and the amount of cash

estimated to be received from customers during the budget period in settlement of their accounts.

One way of preparing a debtors budget is to establish a customer payment pattern, for which purpose guidance may be obtained from the accounting records.

Suppose, for example, that the payment pattern of customers is likely to be as follows:

10% of sales invoices are likely to be paid during the month of invoicing;

70% of sales invoices are likely to be paid during the following month;

20% of sales invoices are likely to be paid during the next month.

These percentages may be applied to the monthly value of sales invoices, which we will assume are as follows:

| Invoices Dated | £ | Source |
|---|---|---|
| November | 150,000 | From sales records or |
| December | 300,000 | previous sales budget |
| January | 300,000 | Assumed phasing of sales |
| February | 300,000 | budget Jan.—March |
| March | 400,000 | |

The budgeted cash to be received from customers may be calculated as shown in Figure 21.

BUDGETED CASH RECEIPTS FROM CUSTOMERS
1st January—31st March

| Invoices Dated | Cash to be received during | | | |
|---|---|---|---|---|
| | Jan. £ | Feb. £ | March £ | Jan.—March £ |
| November (£150,000) | 30,000 (20%) | — | — | 30,000 |
| December (£300,000) | 210,000 (70%) | 60,000 (20%) | — | 270,000 |
| January (£300,000) | 30,000 (10%) | 210,000 (70%) | 60,000 (20%) | 300,000 |
| February (£300,000) | — | 30,000 (10%) | 210,000 (70%) | 240,000 |
| March (£400,000) | — | — | 40,000 (10%) | 40,000 |
| Total | £270,000 | £300,000 | £310,000 | £880,000 |

Figure 21

Figure 21 shows how much cash is likely to be received from

customers month by month, and during the whole of the budget period. Reading across the rows, it will be seen that the estimated cash receipts (£30,000) in respect of November invoices and cash receipts (£270,000) in respect of the December invoices, totalling £300,000 in all, represents the settlement of the opening debtors figure of £300,000, shown in the opening balance sheet at Figure 11.

The remaining rows in the table show the estimated cash receipts in respect of each month's invoices to be rendered to customers during the budget period. Reading down the columns we can discover the amount of cash estimated to be received in total from customers during each month, and during the quarter as a whole, i.e. £270,000 to be received in January, £300,000 in February, £310,000 in March and £880,000 during the quarter as a whole.

Using the information from Figure 21, the debtors budget can now be completed as in Figure 22.

DEBTORS BUDGET
*1st January—31st March*

|  | £ | Source |
|---|---|---|
| Debtors, 1st January | 300,000 | Opening balance sheet (Figure 11) |
| Invoices to be rendered to customers, Jan.—March | 1,000,000 | Sales budget (Figure 12) |
|  | 1,300,000 |  |
| *less* Budgeted cash receipts from customers, Jan.—March | 880,000 | Figure 21 |
| Budgeted debtors, 31st March | £420,000 |  |

Figure 22

The debtors budget shows an estimated increase in the value of customers' accounts outstanding from £300,000 at 1st January to £420,000 at the end of the budget period. (The debtors figure at 31st March may now be inserted by readers in their budgeted balance sheets.)

The significance of this increase in debtors may be assessed later, when changes in the remaining balance sheet figures are known.

*Creditors Budget*

A creditors budget will also be drawn up, and in this case the accountant will probably prepare the budget in co-operation with the buyer. In order to calculate the cash to be paid to creditors during the budget period, percentages may again be used, reflecting the payment pattern of the company in settling its accounts with suppliers.

For illustration purposes we will assume the percentages are as follows:

0% of suppliers' invoices are likely to be paid during the month of invoicing;

70% of suppliers' invoices are likely to be paid during the following month;

30% of suppliers' invoices are likely to be paid during the next month.

These percentages may be applied to the monthly value of purchases invoices, which we assume are as follows:

| Invoices Dated | £ | Source |
|---|---|---|
| November | 200,000 | From purchases records or previous |
| December | 200,000 | purchases budget |
| January | 200,000 | Assumed phasing of purchases |
| February | 300,000 | budget Jan.—March |
| March | 355,000 | |

The budgeted cash payments to suppliers can now be calculated as shown in Figure 23.

BUDGETED CASH PAYMENTS TO SUPPLIERS
1st January—31st March

| Invoices Dated | Cash to be paid during | | | |
|---|---|---|---|---|
| | Jan. £ | Feb. £ | March £ | Jan.—March £ |
| November (£200,000) | 60,000 (30%) | — | — | 60,000 |
| December (£200,000) | 140,000 (70%) | 60,000 (30%) | — | 200,000 |
| January (£200,000) | — (0%) | 140,000 (70%) | 60,000 (30%) | 200,000 |
| February (£300,000) | — | — (0%) | 210,000 (70%) | 210,000 |
| March (£355,000) | — | — | — (0%) | — |
| | £200,000 | £200,000 | £270,000 | £670,000 |

Figure 23

Again, it will be seen, reading across the rows, that £60,000 is estimated to be paid during the quarter in settlement of outstanding November invoices, and £200,000 in respect of outstanding December invoices, making £260,000 in all, which clears the £260,000 creditors' figure in the opening balance sheet (Figure 11).* The remaining rows in the table show the cash estimated to be paid in settlement of January and February suppliers' invoices with no settlement of March invoices during the budget period. Reading down the columns, the table shows the estimated cash payments month by month and during the quarter as a whole.

The creditors' budget can now be completed (Figure 24).

CREDITORS BUDGET
*1st January—31st March*

|  | £ | Source |
|---|---|---|
| Creditors, 1st January | 260,000 | Opening balance sheet (Figure 11) |
| Invoices to be received from suppliers, Jan.—March | 855,000 | Purchases budget (Figure 16) |
|  | 1,115,000 |  |
| *less* Budgeted cash payments to suppliers, Jan.—March | 670,000 | Figure 23 |
| Budgeted creditors, 31st March | £445,000 |  |

Figure 24

The creditors budget shows an estimated increase in suppliers' accounts outstanding from £260,000 at 1st January to £445,000 at 31st March. Again, the significance of the increase in creditors may be assessed later. (The creditors figure at 31st March may now be inserted by readers in their budgeted balance sheets, and the current liabilities at 31st March totalled.)

## Cash Budget

The budgeted cash receipts from customers and the budgeted cash payments to suppliers will form part of the flow of money into and out

---

* Note: Creditors are assumed to be all in respect of goods purchased.

of the company's bank account during the budget period. Starting with the opening cash position of £100,000 as shown in the opening balance sheet at Figure 11, the accountant can prepare a preliminary schedule showing the balance of cash likely to be available to make other payments during the budget period.

CASH BUDGET

*1st January—31st March*

|  | £ | Source |
|---|---|---|
| Cash balance, 1st January | 100,000 | Opening balance sheet (Figure 11) |
| Budgeted cash receipts from customers, Jan.—March | 880,000 | Figure 21 |
|  | 980,000 |  |
| *less* Budgeted cash payments to suppliers, Jan.—March | 670,000 | Figure 23 |
| Balance available for other payments | £310,000 |  |

Figure 25

The balance of £310,000 will be used for such purposes as to pay taxes; to pay for departmental expenses (wages, salaries, etc.) and to make payments for any additional fixed assets which the company is planning to buy and pay for during the budget period.

We will assume that the company is planning to buy and pay for £25,000 additional fixed assets in January. (A new cumulative figure of fixed assets may now be entered by readers in the valuation or cost column of their budgeted balance sheets, and the net fixed assets at 31st March calculated).

Of course such a decision to buy additional fixed assets would require careful assessment before company funds were committed. Techniques for carrying out such an assessment will be discussed in the following chapter.

The cash budget for the period may now be completed as in Figure 26.

CASH BUDGET (cont.)
*1st January—31st March*

| | £ | Source |
|---|---|---|
| Balance available for other payments | 310,000 | Figure 25 |

| | £ | | |
|---|---|---|---|
| *less* Additional fixed assets to be bought and paid for in January | 25,000 | | See text above |
| Tax (see note 1) | 90,000 | | Opening balance sheet (Figure 11) |
| Marketing expenses, excluding depreciation (see note 2) | 45,000 | | Departmental expenses budget (Figure 18) |
| Administration expenses, excluding depreciation (see note 2) | 140,000 | 300,000 | Departmental expenses budget (Figure 18) |
| Budgeted Cash Balance, 31st March | | £10,000 | |

*Notes*

1. For the purpose of illustration, the opening tax liability, shown in the opening balance sheet at £90,000, is assumed to be all paid in January.
2. Depreciation is excluded from the marketing and administration expenses figures in the cash budget because it does not represent an outflow of cash: it is a non-cash expense. It is assumed that all other departmental expenses relating to the budget period will in fact be paid for during the budget period.

Figure 26

The cash budget at Figure 26 shows that if the company goes ahead as planned, the cash balance will be reduced from £100,000 at 1st January to £10,000 at 31st March. (The cash balance at 31st March may now be entered by readers in their budgeted balance sheets, and the current assets at 31st March totalled).

In addition to knowing this over-all change, it is also important to know how the cash figure is likely to fluctuate during the budget period. It is particularly important to know if the company is likely to go into overdraft at any time during the period January/March. If this is the case, the accountant will require to be forewarned, so that the necessary arrangements for an adequate overdraft facility may be made. A phased cash budget is therefore required, showing the balance of cash month by month. Figure 27 provides an illustration of a monthly phased cash budget, showing the sources from which the figures are taken.

PHASED CASH BUDGET
*1st January—31st March*

|  | Jan. £ | Feb. £ | March £ |
|---|---|---|---|
| Opening balance surplus | 100,000 | — | 35,000 |
| *or* (deficit) | — | (5,000) | — |
| *Receipts* |  |  |  |
| Budgeted cash receipts from customers (Figure 21) | 270,000 | 300,000 | 310,000 |
|  | 370,000 | 295,000 | 345,000 |
| *Payments* |  |  |  |
| Budgeted cash payments to suppliers (Figure 23) | 200,000 | 200,000 | 270,000 |
| Additional fixed assets (Figure 26) | 25,000 | — | — |
| Tax (Figure 26, Note 1) | 90,000 | — | — |
| Marketing expenses (Figure 26) | 15,000* | 15,000* | 15,000* |
| Administration expenses (Figure 26) | 45,000* | 45,000* | 50,000* |
|  | 375,000 | 260,000 | 335,000 |
| Closing balance surplus | — | £35,000 | £10,000 |
| *or* (deficit) | (£5,000) | — | — |

*Assumed monthly phasing of cash expenses

Figure 27

The phased cash budget indicates that the company is likely to require an overdraft by the end of January to the extent of £5,000. Unless the pattern of receipts and payments can be altered, e.g. by delaying payment for the fixed assets or of suppliers' accounts, it will be necessary for the accountant to arrange overdraft facilities at the bank to cover the temporary deficit. The phased cash budget emphasizes the

BUDGETED BALANCE SHEET
*31st March*

| | £'000 | | Valu-ation or cost £'000 | Depreci-ation £'000 | Net £'000 |
|---|---|---|---|---|---|
| SHARE CAPITAL | 400 | FIXED ASSETS | 340 | 95 | 245 |
| (assumed no change) | | (see note) | | | |
| | | | | | |
| RESERVES | | | | | |
| Cumulative retained profit | 280 | | | | |
| (Profit & loss budget, Figure 20) | | | | | |
| | | | | | |
| SHAREHOLDERS' CAPITAL EMPLOYED | 680 | | | | |
| | | | | | |
| CURRENT LIABILITIES | | CURRENT ASSETS | | | |
| £'000 | | | £'000 | | |
| Creditors  445 | | Stock, at cost | 480 | | |
| (Creditors bud-get, Figure 24) | | (Stock budget, Figure 14) | | | |
| | | | | | |
| Dividends  10 | | Debtors | 420 | | |
| (Profit & loss budget, Figure 20) | | (Debtors bud-get Figure 22) | | | |
| | | | | | |
| Tax  20 | | Cash | 10 | | |
| (Profit & loss budget, Figure 20) | 475 | (Cash budget, Figure 26) | | | 910 |
| | 1,155 | | | | 1,155 |

Figure 28

| Note FIXED ASSETS | | £'000 | Source |
|---|---|---|---|
| | Valuation or Cost 1st January | 315 | Opening balance sheet (Figure 11) |
| | Additions, Jan./March | 25 | Cash budget (Figure 26) |
| | Valuation or Cost, 31st March | 340 | |

| | | £'000 | |
|---|---|---|---|
| | Cumulative depreciation to 1st January | 80 | Opening balance sheet (Figure 11) |
| | Depreciation, Jan./March | 15 | Departmental expenses budgets (Figure 18) |
| | Cumulative depreciation to 31st March | 95 | |

Figure 28 (cont.)

relationship between the operational plans of management and the financing of the business. It emphasizes the point that managers, by their actions, can not only bring in cash to the business, but can create the need for cash.

For the purposes of illustration we will assume that temporary finance may be obtained from the bank and that no additional share capital or other form of finance is required during the budget period. (Readers may therefore enter in their budgeted balance-sheets the opening share capital figure. The budgeted balance sheet may now be totalled and agreed with Figure 28.)

## Budgeted Balance Sheet, 31st March

The preceding set of budgets represents the link between the opening balance sheet at 1st January and a budgeted balance sheet at 31st March. The budgeted balance sheet at 31st March is shown at Figure 28, together with the sources from which the figures have been taken.

## Profitability

Readers will have noticed that a number of ratios and percentages have been used in drawing up or assessing the foregoing set of budget accounts, including a stock turnover rate (based on quantities); percentages reflecting likely payment patterns, (similar to debtors' and creditors' turnover ratios); the gross profit percentage to sales; and the net profit percentage to sales.

In addition, now that the budgeted balance sheet has been completed, an overall ratio may be calculated, as a means whereby top management may make an assessment of the profitability of the budget proposals. In Chapter 1, profitability was illustrated measured in terms of the ratio profit/total assets. Following this view, we could, for example, relate the budgeted net profit before tax of £50,000 (Figure 19) to the average total assets employed during the budget period of £1,082,500 (£1,010,000 (Figure 11) + £1,155,000 (Figure 28) ÷ 2). As a percentage, the net profit before tax represents a quarterly rate of return of just over $4\frac{1}{2}\%$, i.e. an annual equivalent of just over 18% rate of return on average total assets employed.

Three months, of course, is a relatively short period of time over which to assess profitability. Nevertheless, the principle remains that if top management felt that the budgeted rate of return was insufficient, e.g. by comparison with previous periods or with comparable businesses, a reappraisal might have to be undertaken of the budget accounts, with the object of budgeting for a higher profit figure and/or a lower assets figure.

*Liquidity*

The budget proposals may also be assessed by top management using the two ratios particularly related to liquidity, outlined in Chapter 1. Some deterioration in the ratios will be noticed, which may need watching in the future.

CURRENT ASSETS : CURRENT LIABILITIES (Current ratio)

| *1st January* | *31st March* |
|---|---|
| 775 : 350 or 2 · 2 : 1 | 910 : 475 or 1 · 9 : 1 |

CASH AND DEBTORS : CURRENT LIABILITIES (Acid test ratio)

| *1st January* | *31st March* |
|---|---|
| 400 : 350 or 1 · 1 : 1 | 430 : 475 or 0 · 9 : 1 |

## "*Where Got, Where Gone*"

Top management may also find it useful to review the budget proposals by means of a "where got, where gone" statement. Such a statement summarizes the proposed changes in the sources of finance and the assets of the company. This statement takes a number of forms in practice, with varying degrees of sophistication, but at its simplest may be prepared by comparing the figures in the opening balance sheet with those in the closing. In this case, therefore, a comparison is made between Figures 11 and 28.

"Where got" refers either to an increase in a source of finance, or to a release of part of the funds invested in assets; "where gone" refers either to an increased investment in assets, or to a reduction in a source of finance, e.g. due to payment of a liability. A comparison of Figure 11 with Figure 28 produces the analysis shown in Figure 29.

| WHERE GOT 1st January—31st March | £'000 | Source Figure 11 £'000 | Figure 28 £'000 |
|---|---|---|---|
| Retained profit | 20 | 260 | 280 |
| Funds retained equal to depreciation allowance | 15* | 80 | 95 |
| Funds retained pending payment of dividend | 10 | 0 | 10 |
| Additional credit from suppliers | 185 | 260 | 445 |
| Reduction in cash | 90 | 100 | 10 |
|  | 320 |  |  |

| WHERE GONE 1st January—31st March | £'000 | Figure 11 | Figure 28 |
|---|---|---|---|
| Additional fixed assets | 25* | 315 | 340 |
| Additional stock | 105 | 375 | 480 |
| Additional credit to customers | 120 | 300 | 420 |
| Reduction in tax liability | 70 | 90 | 20 |
|  | 320 |  |  |

* The increase in net fixed assets, £10,000, has been analysed into its component parts, by separately comparing the valuation or cost columns and the depreciation columns in Figures 11 and 28.

Figure 29

This statement clearly shows the proposed heavy reliance on credit from suppliers as an additional source of funds during the budget period, together with the proposed run down of the cash balance. The statement also highlights the use of funds to build up stocks, to provide additional credit to customers and to reduce the tax liability. To a large extent these are offsetting sources and uses. The statement also shows that the additional fixed assets are almost financed by retained profit.

### Summary

In addition to preparing a profit and loss budget, further budgets have been prepared which related more closely to the finance aspect of future operations. These budgets were for debtors, creditors and cash. The cash budget was also prepared in a phased form.

The preparation of these budgets together with the profit and loss budget enabled the accountant to build up a budgeted balance sheet at 31st March. This led to an overall assessment of the budget proposals by the use of a profitability ratio, liquidity ratios and by the use of a "where got, where gone" statement.

Additional complications found in practice have obviously been omitted from this illustration in the interests of highlighting the essential features of a set of budget accounts, and the way in which the budgets interlock. It is evident, however, even from this simple set of figures, that the preparation of a set of budget accounts involves the whole of the management team in a combined effort; and that the preparation of a company plan for future operations is a comprehensive exercise linking operational plans with their financial implications.

### Production and Storage Activity

If a company manufactured its own products instead of buying them ready-made from an outside source, some changes to the set of budget accounts outlined above would be required. The most important change would be the introduction of budget accounts for the company's production and storage activity.

The main feature of this activity may be represented by the following diagram (Figure 30), drawn up in the form of a "bird's eye view" of the production and storage areas.

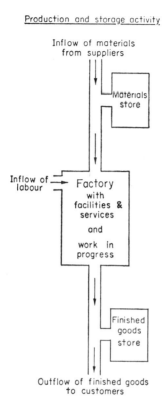

Production and storage activity

Figure 30

The sequence of operations represented by Figure 30 begins with an inflow of materials from suppliers. These materials flow into stock and out again to the factory, the level in the materials store rising and falling according to the balance between factory usage and replenishment.

Materials issued to the factory are worked upon by an inflow of labour, using factory facilities and services (plant and equipment, power supplies, production planning, supervision, etc.) This activity results in semi-finished work in progress in the factory, the level of which may also rise and fall.

Finished goods emerge from the factory, flow into stock and out again to customers; the level in the finished goods store rising and falling according to the balance between factory output and sales to customers. (If some items are not put into stock the flow is, of course, simpler, in that the item in question flows directly down the main limb of the diagram.)

Our task, in the remainder of this chapter, is to see in general terms how a set of budget accounts may be drawn up to reflect this activity in figure form.

### Limiting Factor

An assessment will be required of the limiting factor which is likely to operate during the budget period. As in the previous illustration, three factors of importance are sales, supplies and finance. In the case of a manufacturing company, "supplies" will include the ability of the factory to produce the required output. Factory capacity may therefore act as the limiting factor during the budget period, and this could, in turn, be due to such factors as the availability of a particular type of skilled labour, or the availability of machine capacity to produce the required output. The limiting factor will, of course, set the level of activity to which the other budgets will be geared.

### Factory Output

A budget will be required showing the quantity of finished goods to be produced by the factory during the budget period. For this purpose the production manager will require to establish close liaison with the marketing and stores managers and with the accountant, since the output from the factory is closely related to sales, and the level of stocks.

The basic pattern of the factory output budget may be seen by working up the diagram in Figure 30. The quantity of finished goods to be sold to customers during the budget period will be adjusted for a planned build-up or run-down of stocks in the finished goods store, to equal the required output of finished goods from the factory. The calculations will therefore take the form shown in Figure 31.

A close similarity will be noted between the form of this calculation and the one at Figure 15. (Instead of goods being delivered ready-made from an outside source, goods are now to be delivered ready-made from the factory.) The budgeted figures, as in the earlier illustration, will be the outcome of a number of adjustments reconciling the

|                                  | Quantity units |
| -------------------------------- | -------------- |
| Required for sales               | xxx            |
| Required for closing stock       | xxx            |
|                                  |                |
| Total required                   | xxx            |
| *less* Available from opening stock | xxx         |
|                                  |                |
| Factory output required          | xxx            |

Figure 31

interests of the various managers concerned. For example, the efficiency of the factory may depend upon a steady rather than a fluctuating rate of output. On the other hand, marketing considerations may require a supply of goods which is in line with a varying customer demand. The level of stocks in the finished goods store could perhaps be regarded as a buffer between the requirements of production and the requirements of marketing management; but stores and financial considerations will also mean that the physical volume of finished goods in stock, and the consequent investment of funds, will have to be contained within limits. The preparation of a factory output budget therefore requires a careful assessment and balancing of these various factors, in order to reconcile the interests of the various managers and maximize the over-all company advantage. As in the previous illustration, simpler techniques, such as stock turnover rates, or more sophisticated techniques, such as operational research formulae, may be used to assist in the preparation of the figures.

*Work in Progress*

Where the level of work in progress is likely to build up or run down over the budget period, the amount of factory effort required will not be reflected solely in terms of the budgeted output of finished goods. For example, a build-up of work in progress will require additional effort over and above that required to meet the output figure. Production management should therefore make an estimate of any significant changes which are likely to take place in the level of work in progress, due for example to planned changes in production methods or to a planned increase in capacity utilization.

It may be possible to express such changes in work in progress in terms of the number of equivalent finished units which a planned build-up or run-down represents. For example, assuming that work in progress is considered to be, on average, half finished, a planned build up from 400 semi-finished units to 600 semi-finished units in progress would be equivalent to the production of a further 100 finished units. In this way the factory output budget may be revised up or down, to allow for planned increases or decreases in the level of work in progress.

### Materials, Labour, Factory Facilities and Services

To refer again to Figure 30, the output figure, as adjusted for planned changes in the level of work in progress, implies an inflow of materials from the materials store, an inflow of labour, and the use of factory facilities and services. Consideration will therefore be given to the quantities and types of materials to be used; the numbers, hours of work and grades of the men to be employed; and the various factory facilities and services to be provided. When translated into money terms, these matters form the subject of three cost budgets for the factory: a materials cost budget, a labour cost budget and an overhead cost budget.

### Materials Cost Budget

The preparation of a materials cost budget is greatly facilitated by the existence of standard costs. In principle, the idea of a standard cost is relatively simple; in practice the measurements required are often lengthy and complicated. Basically, a standard material cost is calculated by considering the quantity of material which should be used to produce a unit of finished product, and the price to be paid for the appropriate quality of material. Standard quantity multiplied by standard price equals standard cost.

If such a standard were available, the materials cost budget could be prepared by multiplying the standard materials cost per unit by the number of units to be produced (including an allowance for the equivalent units involved in a change in work in progress levels). Of course, without the existence of such a standard, the problems involved in preparing a materials cost budget would be considerably increased; and in that case, the preparation of a materials cost budget would involve considerations similar to those outlined above in connection with the preparation of the standards themselves.

A cost per unit approach to the preparation of a materials cost budget may not be possible in some businesses, or necessary in others. An alternative would be to try and establish a relationship between materials cost and some other measure of activity, e.g. sales, or the sales value of output. If such a relationship were found to hold good on average, it might be possible to short-cut the preparation of a materials cost budget by simply applying the appropriate percentage to the budgeted figure of activity. Such a method might be sufficiently accurate for the purposes of budget accounts in particular cases; and in any event, such simple average relationships are often useful as quick cross-checks on the results of more detailed calculations.

*Labour Cost Budget*

The preparation of a labour cost budget is also greatly facilitated by the existence of standard costs. A standard labour cost is built up by considering labour time and wage rates: the number of labour hours which should be taken to produce a unit of finished product, and the rate of pay for the appropriate grade of labour. Standard hours multiplied by standard rate of pay equals standard labour cost. The calculations require a careful study of the operations to be performed in the various departments of the factory, the time to be taken and the grade of labour required.

If such a standard is available the labour cost budget may be prepared by multiplying the standard labour cost per unit by the number of units to be produced (including an allowance for work in progress changes). If such a standard is not available, there is again the problem of building up a labour cost budget, requiring considerations similar to those involved in setting labour standards.

In similar fashion to the materials cost budget, the labour cost budget may also be prepared, or cross-checked, by an average percentage relationship between labour cost and an appropriate measure of activity.

*Overhead Cost Budget*

A production overhead cost budget represents the money equivalent of the various factory facilities and services which are to be made available for the achievement of the budgeted production activity. A summary budget will be built up from figures prepared by the various departmental managers. Where appropriate, the costs to be incurred will be calculated in relation to the level of activity budgeted for; and in this connection, the accountant can be of assistance in analysing the behaviour of costs as the level of activity changes, so that costs which are likely to remain fixed in relation to a given variation in activity, are separated from those which are likely to vary with activity, and the rate of change of the latter established. (A further discussion of the analysis of cost behaviour will be found in Chapter 6.) Given a particular planned level of activity, such an analysis should make it easier for the managers concerned to establish budgeted cost figures for their own particular spheres of responsibility.

The overhead cost budget will cover all production costs not included in the materials and labour cost budgets, including such items as management and supervisors' salaries, depreciation of plant and equipment, repairs and maintenance, light and heat, etc.

Having summarized these various figures, the accountant will be able to show the production cost, in terms of materials, labour and overheads, of achieving the required output figure and allowing for planned changes in the level of work in progress. Similarly, he will be able to evaluate the number of semi-finished and finished units to be on hand at the end of the budget period, so creating a budgeted cost of closing work in progress and a budgeted cost of closing stock of finished goods.

*Materials Purchases*

The factors affecting the amount of materials to be purchased during the budget period can be seen by working up the final part of the diagram in Figure 30. The amount of materials to be purchased from suppliers will be based on the requirements of the factory for a flow of materials into production, and on planned changes in the amount of materials to be held in the materials store. The calculation of the required amount of materials to be purchased will, therefore, also be very similar to Figure 15 and is shown in Figure 32 below.

Again, the preparation of these figures will require a reconciliation of the interest of the various managers concerned—the production manager, the stores manager, the buyer and the accountant—in order to maximize the over-all company advantage.

The quantity of materials to be purchased, and the quantity to be held in stock at the end of the budget period, will be evaluated by the accountant, by reference to cost prices of materials, to produce the materials purchases budget and the budgeted cost of closing stock of materials.

|                                        | Quantity units |
| -------------------------------------- | -------------- |
| Required for issue to factory          | xxx            |
| Required for closing stock             | xxx            |
| Total required                         | xxx            |
| less Available from opening stock      | xxx            |
| Purchases required                     | xxx            |

Figure 32

*The Set of Production and Storage Budget Accounts*

A set of production and storage budget accounts may now be prepared from the foregoing. Although having a somewhat complicated appearance when assembled together, it should be remembered that these budgets are simply a reflection, in money terms, of the production and storage activity outlined at Figure 30. Figure 33 overleaf not only summarizes the various budget accounts, but also shows opposite each account heading the equivalent stage reached in the production and storage activity diagram.

*Conclusion*

Further budget preparation will proceed in a similar fashion to the scheme outlined in the earlier part of this chapter. The cost of goods to be sold during the budget period will be deducted from the sales budget figure to produce a budgeted gross profit. Further budgets for departmental expenses, net profit, taxes, dividends, retained profits, debtors, creditors and cash will be prepared, leading to a budgeted balance sheet. The budgeted cost of closing stocks—of materials, work in progress and finished goods—will each appear under the heading of current assets in the budgeted balance sheet.

In conclusion, it should be noted that although this explanation, and the worked examples which preceded it, have traced through a sequence, it should not be assumed, either that this is the only sequence which could be adopted in practice, or that the preparation of a set of budget accounts is in any way a mechanical operation. Budget preparation obviously has to follow an order, but in practice different parts will proceed in parallel, and there will be a good deal of flexibility in operation, as figures prepared previously are adjusted and readjusted in the light of subsequent calculations. Of course, individual businesses will also develop other ways of calculating particular figures to suit their own particular circumstances.

Summaries relating to material contained in earlier sections of this chapter will be found at pages 36 and 48.

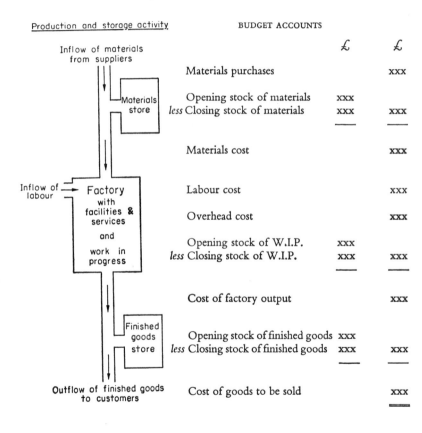

| Production and storage activity | BUDGET ACCOUNTS | £ | £ |
|---|---|---|---|
| Inflow of materials from suppliers | Materials purchases | | xxx |
| Materials store | Opening stock of materials | xxx | |
| | *less* Closing stock of materials | xxx | xxx |
| | Materials cost | | xxx |
| Inflow of labour → Factory with facilities & services | Labour cost | | xxx |
| | Overhead cost | | xxx |
| and work in progress | Opening stock of W.I.P. | xxx | |
| | *less* Closing stock of W.I.P. | xxx | xxx |
| | Cost of factory output | | xxx |
| Finished goods store | Opening stock of finished goods | xxx | |
| | *less* Closing stock of finished goods | xxx | xxx |
| Outflow of finished goods to customers | Cost of goods to be sold | | xxx |

Figure 33

# 3 PLANNING FOR PROJECTS

In the previous chapter we assumed that the company concerned was planning to pay for additional fixed assets to the extent of £25,000 during the budget period. This payment would be the result of an earlier decision to invest in a project, and we must now look more closely at project planning, and in particular at those techniques of analysis which can assist managers to identify profitable projects before they commit the funds at their disposal.

The importance of careful planning needs little emphasis, since projects which involve the acquisition of such long-lived assets as buildings, and plant and equipment, together with associated current assets such as stocks, will obviously affect the profit-earning capacity of a business for some time to come. Furthermore, a management team which finds that it has made a faulty project decision may well be faced with a loss if it is later to sell out and recover its mistake.

This does not, of course, imply that techniques of analysis are adequate by themselves to indicate which course of action to follow in the planning of projects. Managerial judgment will always be needed to a greater or lesser degree, and some projects such as medical and welfare facilities will be judged largely on qualitative considerations. But many business projects give rise to a measurable financial advantage, and it is here that analysis can highlight the likely financial outcome of the proposal and focus attention on the areas where judgment needs to be exercised.

The likely financial outcome of a project is usually measured in three ways: the amount of surplus money it is expected to create, the percentage return on investment it is expected to earn, and the number of years that will be needed to recover the investment in the project. These numbers are called the project's present value, its earning power (also called "internal rate of return" or "discounted cash flow rate of return", or "discounted cash flow yield"), and its pay-back period, respectively. The methods used to calculate these numbers will be explained in this chapter, and the principles brought out by means of simple examples. In addition, two ideas which are basic to all modern approaches to project evaluation will be explained: cash flow and discounting.

*Cash Flow in Project Evaluation*

One of the consequences of implementing a project is that more or less cash will change hands (the word "cash" covers not only coins and notes, but cheques and banking instruments as well). A manager who is sponsoring a project will need to prepare a forecast of these movements of cash, showing how the project is likely to affect the bank account of his organization.

A project can affect the organization's bank account in four possible ways:

(i) It can cause more cash to flow out of the bank account, e.g. additional fixed assets and stocks may need to be bought, and additional operating expenses and taxes paid for.

(ii) It can cause less cash to flow into the bank account, e.g. existing income may be sacrificed, as when a project involves taking an existing product off the market.

These first two changes (more cash out and less cash in) make up a project's negative cash flow.

On the positive side:

(iii) The project can cause more cash to flow into the bank account, e.g. because of additional sales of products, or because of sales of unwanted assets.

(iv) The project can cause less cash to flow out of the bank account, e.g. because of savings in operating expenses and other costs; or because of additional tax allowances enabling tax payments to be reduced.

These last two changes (more cash in and less cash out) make up a project's positive cash flow.

Notice particularly the use of the words "more" and "less" in the definition of a project's cash flow. Only the *changes* caused by the project are being considered in order to see if these additional cash effects are wanted. This means that any cash flows that have already happened, and any cash flows which would happen anyway, should be omitted, since neither can be regarded as changes caused by the project.

Figure 34 provides a simple illustration of a project's negative and positive cash flows, laid out in a form suitable for subsequent analysis.

|  | Cash flow £ |
|---|---|
| Now | − 1,000 |
| Year 1 | + 400 |
| Year 2 | + 600 |
| Year 3 | ⏐ 300 |

Figure 34

This shows a project with a negative cash flow initially, followed by three years of positive cash flow.

*Discounting in Project Evaluation*

The second idea which is basic to all modern approaches to project evaluation is discounting. Discounting is a technique which brings out the importance of the timing of cash flows resulting from a project. We can readily appreciate the importance of timing if we ask ourselves, as private individuals, would we rather have £1 now, or £1 in a year's time?

We would of course prefer to have £1 now. This would be true even if there were no inflation, since we could either spend the £1 immediately rather than wait for a year; or use it to pay off a loan, and so save interest during the year; or invest it at a rate of interest and receive back more than £1 at the end of the year.

Suppose, however, that we were offered the alternative of investing £1 now at 10% per annum, and recovering the £1 plus interest at the end of one year; *or* receiving £1·10 in one year's time. Ignoring tax and the possibility of inflation during the year, we would find either of these alternatives equally attractive, since £1 now invested at 10% will become £1·10 in one year's time. This equivalence may be expressed in two ways:

1. reading forwards in the diagram at Figure 35, overleaf, £1 invested now, at 10%, for 1 year, becomes £1·10; or

2. reading backwards in the diagram, £1·10 receivable 1 year hence, discounted at 10%, has a now, or present value, of £1.

The second approach, which establishes the present value of a sum receivable in the future, is simply the opposite of the more familiar

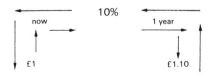

Figure 35

compound interest approach. The present-value approach is also per-haps more familiar than appears at first sight, since it is very similar to the type of calculation performed by a life assurance company when arriving at the surrender value of an endowment policy; the company establishes a present value equivalent to the sum which it would otherwise have paid out on maturity date.

The present values of future sums can be found from interest tables. Figure 36 is an extract from such a table showing the present value of £1 delayed for various numbers of years, up to 10 years hence, using four different rates of discount: 5%, 10%, 14% and 15%.

PRESENT VALUE OF £1<br>(Delayed 1—10 years hence)

| Year | Rate of discount | | | |
|---|---|---|---|---|
| | 5% | 10% | 14% | 15% |
| 1 | ·952 | ·909 | ·877 | ·870 |
| 2 | ·907 | ·826 | ·769 | ·756 |
| 3 | ·864 | ·751 | ·675 | ·658 |
| 4 | ·823 | ·683 | ·592 | ·572 |
| 5 | ·784 | ·621 | ·519 | ·497 |
| 6 | ·746 | ·564 | ·456 | ·432 |
| 7 | ·711 | ·513 | ·400 | ·376 |
| 8 | ·677 | ·467 | ·351 | ·327 |
| 9 | ·645 | ·424 | ·308 | ·284 |
| 10 | ·614 | ·386 | ·270 | ·247 |

Figure 36

In Figure 36, the present values get smaller as the waiting time lengthens, and as we have seen, this reflects the way we feel about receiving or saving cash in the future: the longer the delay, the less is the advantage to us.

But suppose we have to pay cash or sacrifice cash in the future. In this case we would prefer to pay £1 in one year's time rather than pay £1 now. This would be true even if there were no inflation, simply because, by delaying, we can either invest the cash meanwhile, if we already have it, and so earn some interest; or, if we do not have the cash, we avoid early borrowing and so save interest. Figure 36, with its present values getting smaller as the waiting time lengthens, reflects this preference for paying or sacrificing cash later rather than sooner: the longer the delay, the less is the sacrifice.

In summary, we can say that delay reduces both the advantage of positive cash flows and the disadvantage of negative cash flows, so that in the evaluation of a project, whether the future cash flows are positive or negative, they are discounted to smaller figures.

This leads us to consider the calculation of a project's present value.

*Present Value*

We will assume for the purposes of illustration that two projects are to be considered, both requiring an initial investment of £1,000 and both yielding a positive cash flow of £1,300 over their three-year lives. The only difference between these projects is that project A brings cash back sooner than project B (an additional £100 is forecast to be received in year 1 instead of in year 2). The cash flows for each project are as shown in Figure 37.

|  | PROJECT A | | | PROJECT B | | |
|---|---|---|---|---|---|---|
|  | Cash flow | Discount factor | Present value | Cash flow | Discount factor | Present value |
|  | £ | 10% | £ | £ | 10% | £ |
| Now | −1000 | 1·000 | −1000 | −1000 | 1·000 | −1000 |
| Year 1 | + 400 | 0·909 | + 364 | + 300 | 0·909 | + 273 |
| Year 2 | + 600 | 0·826 | + 496 | + 700 | 0·826 | + 578 |
| Year 3 | + 300 | 0·751 | + 225 | + 300 | 0·751 | + 225 |
|  | Net present value | | + 85 | Net present value | | + 76 |

Figure 37

We will also assume that both projects are required to earn at least a 10% rate of return to justify the utilization of the necessary finance and to allow for risk. We find from the table, under the 10% column, the present values of £1 receivable one, two and three years hence.

These present values are listed in the discount factor column of Figure 37. The cash flows are then brought back to their present value equivalents by multiplying by the appropriate discount factor. The initial investment of £1,000 for each project is not discounted because it is already at present value, i.e. it is the amount required now to initiate the project.

Project A has the higher net present value (+ £85 as compared with + £76 for project B) and this is entirely due to the timing of the cash flows in the first two years. In this case, the company concerned would rather receive an additional £100 in year 1 under project A than an additional £100 in year 2 under project B. Notice also that, even though the cash flows have been discounted at 10%, the discounted figures still show a surplus over the outlays. This indicates that both projects are estimated to earn more than the 10% rate of return used in the calculation.

The present-value method is useful to managers in answering two types of question concerning future projects:

1. Is the project likely to earn more than the rate of return used in the calculation? (The answer is yes, if the net present value of the project is greater than zero.)

2. Assuming that projects A and B are alternatives and both satisfy 1. above, which one is to be preferred on financial grounds? (Generally speaking, the project with the higher net present value is to be preferred.)

In the above calculations, 10% was assumed to be the minimum rate of return which the projects must earn to be financially justifiable. This rate must be sufficient to justify the utilization of the necessary finance and allow for risk. As we have seen in previous chapters, companies finance their operations from a variety of sources, including share capital, retained profits, and debentures, so that the calculation of this minimum acceptable rate may be a complicated one in practice, taking into account a weighted average cost of various sources, and the particular risks associated with particular projects. It is likely, however, that the accountant will calculate a basic rate, which can be used throughout the company as a starting point in the decision as to an appropriate rate for a particular project.

*Earning Power*

The object of this calculation is to find the percentage rate of return which a project is likely to earn over its useful life, basing the calculation on the concept of present values. In discussing present values at Figure 37, we noted that both projects were estimated to earn more than a 10% rate of return, i.e. that a positive net present-value figure indicates an estimated rate of return on a project in excess of the rate of discount used in the calculation. Equally, a negative net present-value figure indicates a rate of return lower than that used in the calculation. It follows, therefore, that a net present-value figure of zero indicates a rate of return exactly equal to the rate used in the calculation. This is the basis of an earning power calculation, which finds the rate of discount which will result in a zero figure of net present value, and this is the rate of return which a project is estimated to earn over its useful life.

Using the figures from the previous illustration, and continuing to assume that the projects are estimated to have useful lives of three years, the calculations are as in Figure 38.

#### PROJECT A

|        | Cash flow £ | Discount factor 10% | Present value £ | Discount factor 15% | Present value £ |
|--------|------------|---------------------|-----------------|---------------------|-----------------|
| Now    | − 1000     | 1·000               | − 1000          | 1·000               | − 1000          |
| Year 1 | + 400      | 0·909               | + 364           | 0·870               | + 348           |
| Year 2 | + 600      | 0·826               | + 496           | 0·756               | + 454           |
| Year 3 | + 300      | 0·751               | + 225           | 0·658               | + 197           |
|        |            | Net present value   | + 85            | Net present value   | − 1             |

#### PROJECT B

|        | Cash flow £ | Discount factor 10% | Present value £ | Discount factor 14% | Present value £ |
|--------|------------|---------------------|-----------------|---------------------|-----------------|
| Now    | − 1000     | 1·000               | − 1000          | 1·000               | − 1000          |
| Year 1 | + 300      | 0·909               | + 273           | 0·877               | + 263           |
| Year 2 | + 700      | 0·826               | + 578           | 0·769               | + 538           |
| Year 3 | + 300      | 0·751               | + 225           | 0·675               | + 203           |
|        |            | Net present value   | + 76            | Net present value   | + 4             |

Figure 38

In the above calculations, two different rates of discount have been tried, starting with 10%, to find the one which results most nearly to a net present value of zero. If we approximate to the nearest one per cent, these rates are: 15% for project A and 14% for project B, when the net present values in both cases are about zero.

Having established a rate of return for a project in this way, it could then be used to decide whether or not the project is justifiable financially, by comparing it with whatever minimum acceptable figure is set by top management. (In this particular illustration, the rates of return could also be used to rank the projects in order of priority, but this may not always be the case.)

The rate of return we have calculated is the return on the *outstanding* investment in a project year by year. The idea of a rate of return on the outstanding investment can be illustrated as in Figure 39, by taking the case of project A, where the earning power was found to be almost 15%.

This type of calculation is also more familiar than may appear at first sight. It is very similar to the calculation performed by a building

PROJECT A
(Estimated 3-year life)

|  | £ |
|---|---|
| Outlay | 1,000 |
| add 15% return on £1,000 | 150 |
|  | 1,150 |
| less Cash flow year 1 | 400 |
| Outstanding investment, end year 1 | 750 |
| add 15% return on £750 | 112 |
|  | 862 |
| less Cash flow year 2 | 600 |
| Outstanding investment, end year 2 | 262 |
| add 15% return on £262 | 38 (approx)★ |
|  | 300 |
| less Cash flow year 3 | 300 |
| Outstanding investment, end year 3 | 0 |

★ Includes adjustment for error, due to rounding off to nearest 1%.

Figure 39

society, where the £1,000 outlay would be equivalent to a loan to a borrower, with interest added year by year on the amount of the loan still outstanding, the calculation allowing for the fact that each year's instalment has represented part repayment of the loan and part interest.

## Pay-Back Period

The object of this calculation is to find out the period of time which must elapse before the investment in a project is fully recovered. The investment in a project can be regarded either as the amount invested in it initially, or the initial investment plus interest on the outstanding investment year by year. A pay-back calculation based on the former produces a simple pay-back period; while the calculation based on the latter produces a discounted pay-back period.

The calculation of the simple pay-back period is illustrated for both Projects A and B in Figure 40.

|  | PROJECT A | PROJECT B |
|---|---|---|
|  | Cash flow £ | Cash flow £ |
| Now | − 1,000 | − 1,000 |
| Year 1 | + 400 | + 300 |
| Position after 1 year | − 600 | − 700 |
| Year 2 | + 600 | + 700 |
| Position after 2 years | 0 ←Pay Back→ (end of year 2) | 0 |

Figure 40

Both projects have a simple pay-back period of 2 years, after which the positive cash flow just equals the initial investment of £1,000.

The above calculation may be criticized because it ignores interest on the outstanding investment in the project year by year: that a true pay-back is reached only when both the initial investment *and* interest have been recovered. In order to find out how many years are needed to achieve this state of affairs, the figures need to be re-worked. This time, present-value figures are used.

Figure 41 shows the calculation of the discounted pay-back period for Project A, using data taken from Figure 37. A 10% discount factor is being used, indicating that a 10% rate of interest is to be recovered on the outstanding investment in the project, year by year, in addition to recovery of the initial investment.

PROJECT A

Present value
(10% discount factor)

| | £ |
|---|---|
| Now | − 1,000 |
| Year 1 | + 364 |
| | |
| Position after 1 year | − 636 |
| Year 2 | + 496 |
| | |
| Position after 2 years | − 140 |
| Year 3 | + 225 |
| | ——— Pay back |
| Position after 3 years | + 85 (during year 3) |

Figure 41

Notice how the pay-back period now extends beyond 2 years. Assuming that the cash flow of year 3 accrues evenly through the year, the discounted pay-back period will occur just after $2\frac{1}{2}$ years have elapsed ($2\frac{140}{225}$ years). This is the period of years needed to recover the £1,000 initial investment *and* interest, at the rate of 10%, on the outstanding amount invested in the project year by year.

It should be noted that pay-back calculations, whether simple or discounted, say nothing about what happens to the cash flow after the pay-back period has been reached. Whether these cash flows are a lot or a little and whether they continue for a long time or a short time, the pay-back period is unaffected. Pay-back calculations, therefore, are *not* a measure of the overall profitability of a project.

Their usefulness lies in helping to assess certain kinds of risk. For example, a company may be short of cash and may have limited access to additional finance: in such circumstances the company may prefer to undertake projects which pay back their outlay quickly, in order to minimize the risk of insolvency. Similarly, a company which is operating in a rapidly changing environment, because of changes in the design of the equipment it uses, or of changes in consumer tastes and preferences regarding the product it sells, may prefer to select projects with relatively short pay-back periods in order to minimize the risk of being left holding obsolete assets.

## Some Further Points

Because project planning requires a look ahead over several years, many of the figures used in the calculations will be uncertain. In such circumstances it is useful to make a number of different assumptions concerning the project's cash flows and see the effect of different figures on the project's present value, earning power and pay-back period. For example, the effect of variations in sales volume, sales price and selected cost items could be investigated. Similarly, the effect of a delay in the start up of a project could be studied. It is sometimes the case that what appear to be relatively minor changes in the forecasts can have an important effect on a project's financial outcome; and this is well worth knowing so that managerial judgment can be focused on these key aspects of the proposal.

One particular uncertainty may be the rate of inflation during the life of the project. The word "inflation" can refer to general price increases affecting the organization's financiers, or to the specific price increases affecting the cash flow of the project in question. These latter can be divided into price increases affecting cost items, e.g. wages, salaries, raw materials, each of which may inflate at different rates; and selling price increases, which may inflate at a different rate yet again. If these various rates of inflation are at all significant, they should be built into the calculation; and this could be an especially important point in correctly calculating the taxation effects of a project. Otherwise all calculations will be based on today's prices, which assume either no inflation or that the effects of inflation will be negligible.

Finally, it should be noted that project evaluation is part of a larger scheme of financial analysis, which can be summarized as follows:

$$\text{Ex-post audit} \rightarrow \text{Project evaluation} \rightarrow \text{Overall budgeting}$$

An ex-post audit, which precedes project evaluation, is a systematic review of a past project, in which the forecasts previously made are compared with the results actually achieved. This is something which is not always easy to carry out, e.g. because the accounting system may not always record information by projects, so that results may be difficult to get at. Sometimes it is impossible to check certain figures because they relate to "what might have been". For example, if a project involves withdrawing a product from the market and replacing it with a new one, no one will ever know what the sales of the old product would have been. Despite these difficulties and gaps in information, it is worth attempting an ex-post audit in order to learn as much as possible from experience, before making another project evaluation, and so help to avoid repeating bias and error.

Project evaluation is followed by overall budgeting, in which the effects of each project being considered form part of the balance sheet budget, the profit and loss budget and the cash budget. An analysis of balance sheet and profit and loss budgets may lead to the conclusion that, however desirable the projects may have been when looked at individually, some of them will have to be deferred or even abandoned because of their likely overall impact on the published accounts. Similarly, an analysis of the organization's cash budget may cause some projects to be deferred or abandoned, simply because they cannot all be afforded at once.

*Summary*

Three calculations of assistance to managers who are involved in the planning of future projects have been outlined in this chapter: present value ( a sum of money); earning power (a percentage); and pay-back period (a period of years). Present value and earning power were seen to be indicators of the overall financial attractiveness of the project, while pay-back was seen as a useful supplement to help assess certain kinds of risk. We also noted the desirability, in the face of uncertainty, of basing calculations on various assumptions concerning the future; and also noted some of the issues raised by inflation. Finally we saw how project evaluation is part of a larger scheme of final analysis involving ex-post audits and overall budgeting as well.

# 4 MEASURING PERFORMANCE

So far we have been concerned with the use of accounting figures by managers and the part played by accounting in analysing a business situation and planning for the future. We have considered how figures are calculated only in order to ensure a proper use and understanding of the techniques discussed. In this chapter we now look at some of the more general aspects of accounting measurement which a manager should know about in order to make proper use of information which may be provided by an accountant. We will also look at some of the important features of an accounting system which is designed to help managers, by providing useful comparisons between performance and plan. We will discuss important principles and conventions of accounting, but lay particular emphasis on areas in accounting measurement which require the exercise of judgment: where accounting becomes much more than an application of set rules, and where there is often no one "right" way of measuring.

A key figure in the measurement of performance is the amount of net profit earned during a particular period of time. As we saw in Chapter 2 (Figures 17 and 19), net profit is measured by deducting the cost of goods sold and the expenses incurred in running the business from the revenue earned during a particular period of time. Our first objective, therefore, will be to understand some of the important principles and judgments which lie behind figures of revenue, cost of goods sold and expenses.

*Revenue*

For most businesses, revenue is earned by making sales; and the sales figure is usually arrived at by adding together cash sales and credit sales. Cash sales are recorded at the point of receipt of the cash; but credit sales are not usually recognized at this point, but on the date of the sales invoice. The figure of credit sales will therefore be the total value of sales invoices, whether or not these invoices have been paid by customers during the period under consideration. As we saw in Chapter 2, Figure 28, sales invoices which remain unpaid at the end of the period (and are considered good debts) will be shown as current assets in the balance sheet, representing customers' accounts which it is anticipated will shortly be turned into cash.

For most businesses this way of calculating sales income is reasonably straightforward and is consistently applied. However, we should note in passing that certain types of business may adopt particular ways of measuring their sales for the period. Perhaps the best known of these is in the contracting industry, where individual contracts may take several accounting periods to complete. Rather than wait until the end of a contract before recognizing that revenue has been earned, it is usually the practice to make an interim estimate of revenue earned to date, by considering the degree of completion on the contract.

### Cost of Goods Sold and Expenses

The net profit for the period is found by matching the cost of the goods sold and the expenses for the period, against a figure of revenue; and deducting the total of costs and expenses from the revenue. Matching implies that like should be deducted from like, so that the cost of goods sold, the expenses and the revenue should be calculated on similar bases. The accountant will therefore generally record costs and expenses as they are incurred, rather than wait until they are paid for; and costs and expenses which are unpaid at the end of the period, including unpaid suppliers' invoices, will be shown as current liabilities in the balance sheet as, for example, we saw in Figure 28 of Chapter 2.

This principle of matching the cost of goods sold and the expenses for the period with the figure of revenue is basically an attempt to compare like with like in arriving at a figure of profit; but there are sometimes considerable difficulties and judgments involved in deciding just what constitutes the cost of goods sold and the expenses for the period.

In order to calculate the cost of goods sold, for example, the accountant must first decide what to include in the term "cost". For a trader, the obvious cost is the purchase price of the goods he buys, but it might also be argued that such costs as buying, inward freight and handling are also part of the cost of acquiring goods and making them ready for sale, and should therefore be included in the cost of goods sold figure.

For a manufacturing company, such considerations will particularly affect the way in which materials and components are costed; but the accountant of a manufacturing company is faced with a more fundamental decision as well: the problem of deciding how to calculate the cost of goods made. This problem may be seen by considering the following set of figures for a company which has made 100 units of product during a particular period.

|                            | Costs Incurred £ |
| -------------------------- | ---------------: |
| Direct Costs*              | 1,000            |
| Fixed Production Costs     | 1,800            |
| Administration Department  | 700              |
| Marketing Department       | 600              |
| Total                      | £4,100           |

## Full Cost

Having made 100 units of product, an immediate problem arises as to an appropriate value for those units. One approach would be to consider that the full production costs, direct plus fixed, represent the costs of making the 100 units of product. These costs, it could be argued, are incurred in production, so that the 100 units of product which have been made should be valued at £2,800 (direct cost £1,000+fixed production cost £1,800).

As yet none of the units has been sold, so that included in the balance sheet at the end of the period would be 100 units of product in stock, valued at full production cost:

Stock, at cost†    £2,800

It might also be argued that the figures for the administration and marketing departments are in a particular category, in that they represent expenses of being in business, rather than part of the cost of making units of product. The following could therefore appear in the profit and loss account as expenses of the period:

---

\* Production costs which vary directly with the number of units made e.g. cost of raw materials consumed.

† Stock is usually valued in the balance sheet at the lower of cost or market value: hence, we are assuming that cost is lower than market value, as would normally be the case.

|  |  |
|---|---|
| Administration Department | £ 700 |
| Marketing Department | £ 600 |
| Total Expenses | £1,300 |

There being no sales revenue, the loss for the period will be shown in the profit and loss account as £1,300.

## Direct Cost

On the other hand, it could be argued that the fixed production costs should be treated in the same way as the administration and marketing department figures. The argument might be that items such as factory rent and depreciation on factory plant and equipment are likely to continue, perhaps for a considerable time, at their present levels, despite variations in the number of units made. Therefore these items should not be treated as product costs, but as expenses of being in business during the period: they represent the expenses of having a factory, in the same way that the administration department figure, for example, represents the expenses of having an administration.

In this case, only the direct costs are considered to be the consequence of producing 100 units; so that these units will appear in the balance sheet at the end of the period as follows:

|  | £ |
|---|---|
| Stock, at cost | 1,000 |

This would mean that the expenses for the period appearing in the profit and loss account would consist of:

|  | £ |
|---|---|
| Production Department | 1,800 |
| Administration Department | 700 |
| Marketing Department | 600 |
| Total | £3,100 |

There being no sales revenue, the loss for the period under this approach would be £3,100.

It is evident that we cannot say definitely that either method is right and the other wrong; but it is also evident that the two methods can produce different profit or loss figures. This will be so whenever there is a build up or run down of stocks (in the above example there was a build up of 100 units). The two methods will also produce different stock figures for the balance sheet; direct costing always producing the lower figure.

### Cost Per Unit

One advantage of the direct-cost approach is that it eliminates fluctuations in the cost per unit of product. In the above example, 100 units of product were produced at a direct cost of £1,000 or £10 each. Had the output been only 60 units, the direct costs would have fallen to £600, leaving the cost per unit the same at £10.

On the other hand, the full production cost of making 100 units was £2,800, or £28 each. Had the output been only 60 units, the fixed production costs would have remained the same at £1,800, and the full cost of making 60 units would therefore have been £2,400 (fixed production cost £1,800+direct cost £600) or £40 each. This rise in the cost per unit from £28 to £40 is due to the fact that the fixed production costs are being spread over fewer units, so that each unit bears a larger share. Physically identical units of product may therefore be costed at different figures under full costing simply because of volume variations; whereas direct costing avoids this.

An alternative way of avoiding fluctuations in unit cost is to use a predetermined rate for charging units of product with a share of the fixed production costs: each unit of product will then be charged with the same amount of fixed production cost, even though volume of production varies. Perhaps the best known use of a predetermined rate is to be found in a standard costing system, where fixed production costs are charged at a standard rate based on a budgeted volume of production. Any variation which arises because the actual volume of production differs from the budget is highlighted as a volume variance. (A further discussion of this and other variances, and their use by managers for control action, will be found in the following chapter.)

*Changing Cost Levels*

So far we have said nothing about changes in cost figures due to changes in cost levels, i.e. we have ignored the presence of inflation or deflation. To the extent that inflation or deflation occurs, additional problems of accounting measurement arise, which will also affect the calculation of stock values and therefore the figures of cost of goods sold and of profit.

Suppose that items are bought (or made), put into stock and sold during a period when cost prices rise. An extract from the stock account is shown in Figure 42.

| | IN | | | OUT | | BALANCE IN STOCK | |
|---|---|---|---|---|---|---|---|
| | Quantity units | Cost Price | Cost £ | Quantity units | Cost £ | Quantity units | Cost £ |
| Jan. 1 | — | — | — | — | — | 0 | 0 |
| Jan. 10 | 90 | £1·00 | 90 | — | — | 90 | 90 |
| Jan. 20 | 60 | £1·10 | 66 | — | — | 150 | 156 |
| Jan. 25 | — | — | — | 50 | ? | 100 | ? |
| Jan. 31 | — | — | — | — | — | 100 | ? |

Figure 42

By 20th January 150 units are in stock at a total cost of £156. The problem is to calculate the cost of the 50 units sold on 25th January and the cost of the 100 units which remain in stock on 31st January.

*First In First Out (FIFO)*

One approach might be to trace the flow of costs as if they followed the normal physical flow of stock items, assuming that the oldest units are withdrawn first from stock. This first-in-first-out (FIFO) approach would lead to the following figures.

| OUT | | BALANCE IN STOCK | |
|---|---|---|---|
| Quantity units | Cost £ | Quantity units | Cost £ |
| 50 | 50 | 100 | 106 |

Figure 43

The 50 units out are costed as if they were the first 50 units in, i.e. at £1 per unit, leaving a stock of 100 units costed as 40 units at £1 each plus 60 units at £1·10 each, making the total cost of stock £106.

## Last In First Out (LIFO)

An alternative approach might be based on the view that, even though the oldest units may have been drawn out first, the physical flow of goods should not govern the method of costing these units. For accounting purposes, therefore, these units could be costed on a last-in-first-out (LIFO) basis, i.e. the 50 units out could be costed as if they were the most recently acquired items. This LIFO approach would lead to the following figures:

| OUT | | BALANCE IN STOCK | |
|---|---|---|---|
| Quantity units | Cost £ | Quantity units | Cost £ |
| 50 | 55 | 100 | 101 |

Figure 44

The 50 units out will therefore be costed at £1·10; leaving a stock of 100 units, costed as 10 units at £1·10, plus 90 units at £1, making the total cost of stock £101.

## Average Price

Another method would be to cost on a basis of a weighted average price. Figure 42 shows that 150 units have cost a total of £156, so that 50 units will have cost on average £52. Following this view, the stock account would appear as follows:

| OUT | | BALANCE IN STOCK | |
|---|---|---|---|
| Quantity units | Cost £ | Quantity units | Cost £ |
| 50 | 52 | 100 | 104 |

Figure 45

## Current Cost

The above examples have all accounted for the historical cost of the stock items in question. An alternative is to account on a current-cost basis. Under this approach the 50 units out are valued at their current cost at the date of sale; and the 100 units in stock are valued at their current cost on the stock valuation date. Suppose that the current cost is £1·20 per unit at the date of sale (25th January) and £1·25 per unit at the date of the stock valuation (31st January). The current-cost approach will then lead to the following figures:

| OUT | | BALANCE IN STOCK | |
|---|---|---|---|
| Quantity units | Cost £ | Quantity units | Cost £ |
| 50 | 60 | 100 | 125 |

The 50 units out are costed at £1·20 each (the current cost at the date of sale); and the 100 units in stock are costed at £1·25 each (the current cost at the date of the stock valuation).

The examples given of FIFO, LIFO, average-price, and current cost methods have each produced different sets of numbers; nevertheless, each method may be said to represent the money measure of the same physical movement of stocks, and no one figure can be regarded as necessarily right and the others wrong. The different figures in our illustrations have simply reflected different emphases placed in the direction of current cost or historical cost levels in times of inflation.

## Fixed Asset or Expense

We have seen that the distinction between expenditure which results in an asset appearing in the balance sheet, and expenditure which results in an expense appearing in the profit and loss account is an important one affecting the calculation of profit, period by period. When the expenditure is considered to result in a fixed asset, particular problems of accounting measurement arise.

The first problem is to decide how much expenditure represents the original cost of the fixed asset i.e. how much expenditure should be capitalized for balance sheet purposes. General guides would be to capitalize expenditure which is considered to benefit future accounting periods, or to capitalize expenditure which is necessary to place the asset in a working condition, in the location where it is wanted; but practice will inevitably differ in particular cases. Consider, for example, the question of delivery charges on equipment transferred from one location to another, on removal of a business from its present site. It could be argued that because these charges are part of the cost of placing the equipment in its new location, the expenditure should be capitalized, either separately or as part of the cost of the fixed assets removed. On the other hand, a more conservative course of action could be taken, to write off such expenditure to profit and loss account in the period in which the expenditure is incurred, i.e. to charge it as an expense of the period.

Similar problems arise as to whether or not installation costs should be capitalized. If such costs are capitalized, on the grounds that they are incurred in order to get the assets in a working condition, further questions arise, such as whether or not part of the company's own wage and overhead cost should be included, if installation were carried out by the company's own labour force; if so, what items of overhead should be included and how much overhead would be appropriate; and whether the phrase "installation costs" includes such items as costs incurred in removing old equipment, knocking down and rebuilding a wall, or otherwise altering a building, all of which might be necessary in order to make room for, and install, the new equipment.

Problems of definition also arise when overhauls and maintenance programmes are undertaken. The replacement of a few tiles on the roof of an office block would no doubt be considered to be a maintenance item by most people, and charged to the current period's profit and loss account as an expense, but how should we classify the complete re-roofing of a building which is in a dilapidated condition? Could it to some extent represent a backlog of repairs and maintenance inadequately carried out in the past and so charged, in part at least, as an expense; or is it to be considered an improvement and capitalized? General guides might be to capitalize expenditure which is considered to improve the asset beyond its original condition when first bought, or which is considered to extend the economic life of the asset or increase its revenue-earning capacity, but there are obvious difficulties in deciding on an appropriate figure.

*Depreciation*

Assuming that a certain amount of expenditure has been capitalized, so creating a fixed asset in the balance sheet, further decisions must then be made relating to:

1. the useful life of the asset;
2. the scrap or resale value of the asset at the end of its useful life;
3. the method by which depreciation will be calculated.

The useful life of a fixed asset is particularly influenced by three factors: the rate of physical wear and tear; the rate of obsolescence of the asset itself; and the rate of obsolescence of the product or service which the asset helps to produce. Each of these factors must be considered (not necessarily by the accountant alone) to determine which is likely to exert the dominant influence. Estimating the useful life of an asset is, of course, a difficult task, particularly for new types of assets, although for many companies, once a life has been estimated for a particular type, the tendency is to adopt standard periods of time over which similar assets are written off.

The scrap or resale value of the asset at the end of its useful life will also be considered, and if likely to be significant, will be allowed for in determining the amount to be depreciated. Finally, the method of calculating depreciation must be decided upon.

There are several methods available for calculating depreciation, three of which will be illustrated. The methods will be illustrated with reference to a fixed asset which originally costs £2,000, has an estimated useful life of 100,000 hours over a 5 year period, with negligible scrap or resale value at the end of its useful life.

*Straight-Line Method*

One approach is to view the asset as equally available for use over its life, so that an equal amount of depreciation should be written off year by year. The amount to be depreciated is divided by the number of years of useful life to produce the annual depreciation charge. The result in our particular example is to charge the profit and loss account for each year of useful life with depreciation of:

$\frac{£2,000}{5} = £400$. Extracts from the balance sheet, showing the cost and accumulated depreciation figures year by year, using the straight-line method, are given in Figure 46.

BALANCE SHEET (EXTRACT)

| | End Yr 1 £ | End Yr 2 £ | End Yr 3 £ | End Yr 4 £ | End Yr 5 £ |
|---|---|---|---|---|---|
| Cost | 2,000 | 2,000 | 2,000 | 2,000 | 2,000 |
| *less* Depreciation | 400 | 800 | 1,200 | 1,600 | 2,000 |
| Net | £1,600 | £1,200 | £ 800 | £ 400 | £ 0 |

Figure 46

## Reducing Balance Method

Another approach might be to accelerate the rate of depreciation in the early years, on the grounds that this is the time when the asset is most efficient and so more should be charged for its services then. Progressively smaller amounts of depreciation are charged as the asset becomes less useful, because of declining efficiency and the need for more repairs and maintenance. The reducing balance method is one method which achieves this, by applying a constant percentage to the reducing net book value, period by period.

Using 40% as the constant percentage, the calculations are as shown below:

| | £ |
|---|---|
| Cost | 2,000 |
| *less* Depreciation Yr 1 (40% x £2,000) | 800 |
| | 1,200 |
| *less* Depreciation Yr 2 (40% x £1,200) | 480 |
| | 720 |
| *less* Depreciation Yr 3 (40% x £720) | 288 |
| | 432 |
| *less* Depreciation Yr 4 (40% x £432) | 173 |
| | 259 |
| *less* Depreciation Yr 5 (40% x £259, adjusted to write off the asset completely) | 259 |

Figure 47

In contrast to Figure 46, the following figures would be included in the balance sheet if the reducing balance method were adopted:

BALANCE SHEET (EXTRACT)

|  | End Yr 1 £ | End Yr 2 £ | End Yr 3 £ | End Yr 4 £ | End Yr 5 £ |
|---|---|---|---|---|---|
| Cost | 2,000 | 2,000 | 2,000 | 2,000 | 2,000 |
| *less* Depreciation | 800 | 1,280 | 1,568 | 1,741 | 2,000 |
|  | £1,200 | £ 720 | £ 432 | £ 259 | £ 0 |

Figure 48

### Production-Unit/Production-Hour Method

Neither the straight-line nor the reducing balance method relates the periodic charge for depreciation specifically to the rate of usage of the asset. For some fixed assets, including vehicles and certain types of plant and equipment, a fluctuating amount of depreciation based on usage may be more appropriate, so that the more the asset is used, the greater the charge for depreciation. A production-unit or production-hour method of depreciation would achieve this, by applying an estimated rate of depreciation per unit, or per hour, to the usage actually incurred.

In the above example the amount to be depreciated is £2,000 over 100,000 hours, or £0·02 per hour. This rate will be applied to the actual usage incurred during each accounting period, in order to arrive at the periodic depreciation charge.

### Current-Cost Depreciation

The above calculations have all accounted for the historical cost of the asset over its useful life. An alternative is to account on a current-cost basis. Suppose that the asset is subject to price increases (for simplicity, these are assumed to occur at the beginning of each year) and that the amounts on which the calculations are based, each year, are as shown below:

| for year 1 | £2,000 |
|---|---|
| for year 2 | £2,500 |
| for year 3 | £3,000 |
| for year 4 | £3,500 |
| for year 5 | £4,000 |

Using the straight-line method of depreciation, and continuing to assume a 5 year life, the current-cost approach will result in a depreciation charge in the Profit and Loss Account, for each year, of the following amounts:

| Year 1 | Year 2 | Year 3 | Year 4 | Year 5 |
|---|---|---|---|---|
| £ | £ | £ | £ | £ |
| 400 | 500 | 600 | 700 | 800 |
| $\left(\dfrac{£2,000}{5}\right)$ | $\left(\dfrac{£2,500}{5}\right)$ | $\left(\dfrac{£3,000}{5}\right)$ | $\left(\dfrac{£3,500}{5}\right)$ | $\left(\dfrac{£4,000}{5}\right)$ |

Asset values, based on current cost at each year end, will reflect the fraction of the asset's life yet to be used up:

| | Asset value |
|---|---|
| | £      £ |
| End year 1 | $2,000 \times 4/5 = 1,600$ |
| End year 2 | $2,500 \times 3/5 = 1,500$ |
| End year 3 | $3,000 \times 2/5 = 1,200$ |
| End year 4 | $3,500 \times 1/5 = 700$ |
| End year 5 | $4,000 \times 0/5 = 0$ |

*Depreciation and Market Value*

It is particularly important to note that depreciation is *not* a method by which fixed assets are reduced to their market values period by period: depreciation methods intend that market value, if any, will be reached only at the *end* of the useful life. Readers will recall from Chapter 1 that fixed assets are acquired primarily to be kept and used rather than to be sold again, so that it is not generally relevant to consider their market value period by period, unless there is a possibility of selling before the useful life has expired. Of course, the market value of a fixed asset need not equal either its historical cost or its current cost, and this is particularly true of purpose-built fixed assets which have a limited market.

### Apportioning Costs to Time Periods—Further Examples

Much of the discussion in previous sections has been concerned with the problem of apportioning costs to time periods. Within this general theme, further examples may be given.

Suppose that a company acquires a subsidiary at a price which exceeds the fair value of the assets bought. This excess is the price paid for goodwill. Most accountants would record this figure as an asset and write it off over a period of years; but the amount to be written off each year and the number of years over which this is to take place are difficult to determine, and practice will often differ from one company to another. In passing, we may note that the goodwill figure, like fixed assets generally, will not be shown in the balance sheet at market value. It will be shown at cost, less amounts written off to date. The goodwill figure in the balance sheet is therefore not intended to represent what the company would receive for goodwill if its business were sold.

Occasionally, companies may consider carrying forward to a future period part of a particular period's advertising cost. This is an attempt to recognize that a part of the advertising will benefit future accounting periods, and so should be matched against future revenue, rather than all charged as an expense in the current period's profit and loss account. This practice will usually only occur in connection with a major advertising campaign, where substantially more than the normal level of advertising has been incurred. The decision concerning the amount to be carried forward in this way, and the number of accounting periods over which the cost should be apportioned, are also evidently matters of judgment.

A similar situation arises with costs incurred in creating and organizing a business. These costs will benefit future accounting periods, so that a decision may be made to capitalize them, in whole or in part, and write them off over a period of time, rather than write them off entirely in the period in which they are incurred; but because such decisions inevitably depend upon opinion, practice could well differ from one company to another.

*Managerial and Departmental Performance*

Many of the aspects of accounting which we have considered in previous sections will be applicable to the measurement of the performance of managers and their departments. When we consider the performance of a company as a whole, we are also considering the performance of its top managers, since it is they who bear the ultimate responsibility for the over-all results; furthermore, the measurement of the performance of lower levels of management and their departments can be regarded as a part of the total picture. But when we consider the measurement of managerial and departmental performance, it is more important than ever to emphasize that accounting should provide information which is useful to the user: in particular, that accounting information should be suited to the purpose in hand and the person receiving it.

If accounting information for managers is to yield the highest degree of usefulness, the information should, as far as possible, be tailored to the needs of the situation and the needs of the individual manager. As situations and individuals differ, there is therefore likely to be a variety of accounting information prepared for managers, and a variety of methods by which the figures are calculated.

There will also be considerable scope for the exercise of judgment in deciding just what constitutes useful information, so that the problem of selecting the most appropriate way of measuring events for managers extends well beyond the selection of an appropriate accounting technique, to include an assessment of the most appropriate content of the reports presented, and the most appropriate form and frequency of presentation. Managers have a vital role to play in deciding on their information needs: they have a better knowledge than anyone else of the workings of their departments; of the strengths and weaknesses of the system and of their subordinates; of the types of quantitative data which they already have available and find useful; of the kinds of things which may go wrong and need reporting on, or at least watching; of the seriousness of these adverse happenings, e.g. their repercussions elsewhere in the system; and of the earliest point at which they may be spotted.

These and similar matters are of importance in deciding on the content of reports to be prepared by the accountant; on their frequency— whether they are to be *ad hoc* reports or regular, and, if the latter, at what time interval—and on their degree of urgency. This is evidently an area of accounting measurement which managers cannot leave entirely to the accountant, if they are to receive what *for them* is the right quantity of the right type of information, at the right time. Just as managers are involved in planning for future operations and projects, with the aid of the accountant, so, too, they should be involved in the planning of their management accounting reports.

Although the ideal from the user's point of view would be a set of reports tailored to his individual needs, completely tailor-made accounting systems are rarely found in practice. This is due, in no small part, to the cost of operating such systems; and some element of standardization is usually considered desirable in the interests of keeping down the cost of accounting. The cost of the accounting system itself must be justified in terms of the benefit obtained, and a point will come in all accounting systems where the additional benefit obtained from a change is not considered to be worth the additional cost. A question such as "Is a particular report worth producing?" will lead the manager and the accountant, jointly, to attempt a weighing up of the benefit to be obtained from a report against the cost of its preparation—a difficult exercise to undertake, since the former is an intangible and the latter usually an imprecise measurement. Nevertheless, such an exercise is essential, and should be carried out periodically, if managerial and departmental performance is to be measured economically as well as effectively.

One aspect of accounting for the performance of managers and their departments, which is particularly important, is a definition of the responsibilities of the individuals concerned and a decision regarding what constitute controllable items. Unless the figures presented to individuals relate to their own particular responsibilities and are controllable by them, little effective action can be taken following their receipt. A definition of responsibilities and a decision as to which items are controllable by particular individuals is therefore essential, and is the first stage from which individual managers can agree with the accountant on the headings under which information will be collected and reported to them.

If a company operates a system of budgetary control, much of this work may already have been done, since the effective preparation of budgets by individual managers and their departments requires a definition of managerial responsibilities and a classification of accounting headings, to avoid overlapping or omissions in the figures. The classification finally agreed on will be summarized in the form of an accounts code, which is used to code the basic paperwork, forming the input to the accounting system, and which is the basis for the subsequent reports. In passing we should note that it may be quite inadequate to refer to family-tree diagrams or manuals in order to define responsibilities, not only because they may be out of date, but because they may inadequately represent the real set of relationships between people which in fact exist, despite what has been charted or written down.

It is evident that the possible variety of information which might be considered useful and economical, for different managers in different situations, is so great that statements as to the way in which managerial and departmental performance might be reported on can only be general. The difficult task of deciding what information a manager needs in a particular situation is not to be solved simply by looking at specimen reports drawn from other cases in practice, although the content of such reports and their form of presentation may obviously be a stimulus to thought.

The content of management accounting reports will vary according to the number of accounting building-bricks which it is necessary or practicable to assemble together. For example, at the highest level of management an overall profitability figure may be used. This form of measurement may be possible at divisional or branch level of management as well, if the managers are, in effect, put in the position of being in business on their own, and are therefore responsible for earning an adequate rate of return on the assets they employ.

Accounting reports may also be expressed in terms of profit earned, without necessarily relating this figure to assets employed. Both this and the profitability form of measurement may be extended by a system of transfer pricing, whereby one section of a business sells its products or services to another.

For departments such as the sales department, performance may also be measured in terms of revenue earned and expenses incurred. In other cases, such as in the factory or in administration, the appropriate form of measurement may simply be expenses incurred, which may or may not also be capable of expression in terms of a cost per unit of output.

*Product Performance*

The measurement of the performance of individual products or product groups will also involve the application of many of the principles and judgments of accounting, which have been discussed earlier in this chapter. One particular feature of the calculation of product costs or product profits, however, is the apportionment of overheads: a process which is bound to be somewhat arbitrary in practice.

Consider, for example, the case of a company which operates two production departments. Each department incurs certain costs which can be identified as relating specifically to that department, e.g. its own particular labour and material consumption costs. In addition, there will be certain costs which are incurred for the benefit of both departments, e.g. factory rent and works management salaries, which are therefore overheads from the point of view of either department. As a first stage in arriving at product costs, these overheads will be apportioned to the production departments, using bases which, for the particular circumstance of the case, are felt to give a fair share of overhead to each. Factory rent, for example, might be apportioned on the basis of square metres of space occupied, with possibly some weighting for additional amenities enjoyed in one location rather than another. Works management salaries might be apportioned on the basis of the numbers of people employed in each production department, or in proportion to their salaries and wages cost.

The creation of separate service departments, such as a maintenance department, steam and electricity generation, factory personnel department, or a factory canteen, produces further problems of apportionment, in that bases have to be found for arriving at a fair share of the service department costs to be charged to each production department. Measures of usage may be possible, such as labour-time bookings for maintenance work and meter readings for steam and electricity usage. Such measures, although possible, might not always be practicable, so that, for example, it might not be considered worthwhile installing electricity meters in every department of a large factory. In such a case, and in cases where direct measurement of services is impossible, such as with the factory personnel department, fair-share bases for apportionment have to be found.

Service departments which render services to each other create additional problems. For example, the maintenance department might serve the personnel department, which in turn serves the maintenance department. A frequently found solution to this problem is to take each service department in a particular order, and apportion its costs only once.

The process of apportionment described above enables overhead rates to be calculated so that products passing through the various production departments of the business may be charged with a fair share of overhead. Overhead rates are commonly calculated in terms of an amount of overhead per labour or machine hour, or per unit of product. These rates, and the apportionment which lies behind them, are not necessarily related to a production department as a whole, but could relate to a relatively small section of a department, such as a group of machines, or even to a single machine if such a degree of detail were felt to be justified in particular cases.

A manager who is using product cost figures which are based on procedures similar to those described above, will readily appreciate that he is dealing with approximations. In order to obtain a better perspective on the likely degree of approximation in the data he is handling, it is often helpful for a manager to obtain a general understanding of the processes of apportionment carried out in his own company. Furthermore, the individual manager can often assist the accountant in deciding on suitable bases for particular circumstances.

*Joint Products and By-Products*

Before leaving the subject of product costing mention should be made of joint products and by-products, which arise when two or more products are made from the same raw material source, as when parts of an animal yield various meat and skin products. This situation produces considerable problems in accounting measurement, which are something more than extreme forms of apportionment problems, since *any* method of apportionment will be arbitrary.

The costs incurred up to the point of separation may be split according to a number of assumptions, but perhaps the best known methods are to split the cost in proportion to the sales value of the various products produced, or the weight of the various products produced. Joint products are thereafter costed separately as further processing continues, while the value of a by-product is usually regarded as a reduction in the total cost of the main product.

## Summary

In this chapter we have been concerned with ways in which the accountant measures performance, dealing with general principles of accounting measurement, and laying special emphasis on problem areas where there is often no one "right" way of measuring. We have discussed the calculation of revenue, cost of goods sold and expenses, together with related problems in accounting for stocks and fixed assets.

This led us to consider in more detail the measurement of the performance of individual managers and their departments, and to discuss important factors affecting the usefulness of information provided for managers by an accounting system.

Finally we considered the measurement of product performance, and discussed the various calculations which lie behind product cost figures, including the apportionment of overheads and the separation of joint and by-product costs.

# 5 COMPARING PERFORMANCE WITH PLAN

A comparison between performance and plan and the analysis of variances between the two is a preliminary step towards the taking of corrective action by managers: action which in most cases will be aimed at modifying future performance, but may also result in replanning, or improved planning in the future. In this chapter we will consider how the accountant can help managers in this connection, by analysing and reporting on important variances. Our attention will be focused primarily on those techniques which can help to indicate the cause of a variance and the person who is responsible for correcting it.

It should be noted at once that the interpretation of variances can only be carried out by those who are in touch with the particular circumstances of the case, and that further investigations are usually necessary, beyond figure analysis, to find out the underlying causes. It is true that, by virtue of additional information in his possession, the accountant can often add a written explanation to a figure report, so aiding the manager in his interpretation, and introducing an element of flexibility into a reporting system which might otherwise become unduly standardized; furthermore, it is always possible to design an accounting system which can enable the accountant to calculate a variety of variances by cause, so long as the extra benefit to be obtained from this information is considered to be worth the extra cost incurred. But despite this, the manager will inevitably have to fill in a good deal of background detail for himself, including those factors which cannot be measured directly in figure form, such as human relations problems, which may be the basic reason why performance has deviated from plan. This is simply another example of the general point that accounting does not provide all the information (or necessarily the most essential information) which a manager needs in order to make a business decision.

Nevertheless, variance analysis is an essential aid to management, because it focuses attention on the existence of a deviation from plan; on the direction of this deviation (favourable or adverse); and on its extent. Variance analysis throws valuable light on the causes of a problem, and can help to isolate those factors which are controllable by particular individuals. It can focus attention on selected areas of a business and on a limited range of pertinent information, so enabling managers to manage by exception.

It is convenient to divide variance analysis into two main headings: cost variances and sales variances. Cost variances, in turn, may be considered under three headings: labour variances, materials variances and overhead variances.

*Labour Variances*

In Chapter 2 we saw how a standard labour cost was built up by considering labour time and rates of pay: the number of labour hours which should be taken to produce a unit of product, and the rates of pay for the appropriate grades of labour. Standard hours multiplied by standard rates of pay equalled standard labour cost.

If we compare the actual labour cost incurred by a department in producing a certain number of units of product, with the equivalent standard labour cost, we can obtain a wages variance. This variance is favourable if actual labour cost is less than standard, and adverse if it exceeds standard. Useful as it is to know that labour has, in total, cost more or less than it should, if appropriate managerial action is to be taken further analysis is needed with the aim of highlighting the underlying causes of this variance, and indicating who is responsible for taking the necessary corrective action.

Since wages are made up of hours multiplied by rates of pay per hour, the wages variance may be analysed into two components: a labour efficiency variance, which arises when actual time taken differs from standard time set; and a wages rate variance, which arises when actual rates of pay differ from the standard rates set.

Suppose, for example, that the labour cost incurred in a particular department is £21,600 during a particular period, and that the standard labour cost for the number of units produced is £20,000. The wages cost variance is therefore adverse to the extent of £1,600. Analysis of this variance produces the following additional information (Figure 49).

|  | Actual | Standard | Variance |
|---|---|---|---|
| Hours | 4,800 | 5,000 | |
| Rate per hour | £4·50 | £4·00 | |
| Cost | £21,600 | £20,000 | £1,600 (adverse) |

Figure 49

Let us consider the hours component first: the labour force has taken 4,800 hours to do what should have taken 5,000 hours, i.e. there has been an efficiency gain of 200 hours. At the standard rate of £4·00 per hour this represents a favourable labour efficiency variance of £800 (200 hours × £4·00 per hour).

On the other hand, the actual rate per hour (£4·50) has exceeded the standard rate (£4·00) so that the labour force has cost 50p per hour more than was intended. For the 4,800 hours actually worked, this represents an adverse wages rate variance of £2,400 (50p × 4,800 hours).

To summarize:

|  | £ |  |
|---|---|---|
| Labour efficiency variance (200 hours × £4·00 per hour) | 800 | (favourable) |
| Wages rate variance (50p per hour × 4,800 hours) | 2,400 | (adverse) |
| Wages cost variance | £1,600 | (adverse) |

The above variance analysis may also be represented in the form of a diagram, with hours plotted along the x-axis and rates per hour along the y-axis.

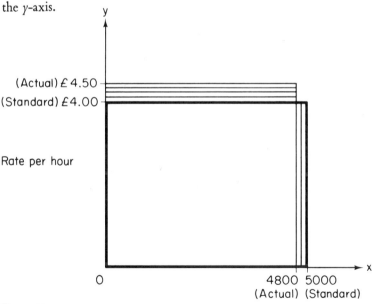

Figure 50

Hours

The variances can be clearly seen as the shaded areas: in the case of the rate variance, actual exceeds standard, so that the adverse variance is measured by the area shaded . (50p per hour × 4,800 hours).

In the case of the efficiency variance, actual hours are less than standard, so that the favourable variance is measured by the area shaded (200 hours × £4·00 per hour) . . . . . . . . .

### Interpretation of Labour Variances

This analysis has revealed the important fact that labour cost has exceeded standard, not because of a falling-off of efficiency (there is in fact an efficiency gain), but because the standard rate of pay per hour has been exceeded. The action which should follow this analysis depends upon the particular circumstances of the case. For example, the labour efficiency variance might form the subject of praise from manager to subordinate for achieving a certain amount of work in less than standard time (a case where accounting aids the motivational aspect of management). The favourable efficiency variance might also suggest to managers that success could be repeated in other, similar, spheres of operation, so focusing attention on the performance of similar departments. Or the variance might be one of a number of favourable variances which have been consistently achieved in the past, and this may indicate that the standard itself is in need of revision, i.e. variance analysis may indicate the need for replanning.

The adverse rate variance might be a non-controllable factor, representing simply a wage award, which has occurred during the period and was not allowed for in drawing up the standard. The variance might, however, be controllable, at least in part, in the sense that local management might be empowered to offer local allowances above standard in order to attract particular grades of labour.

So far we have assumed that the labour efficiency and the wages rate variances are independent. They might, however, be interdependent, in the sense that the favourable efficiency variance could be the consequence of the adverse rate variance. Such a situation could arise where a manager or his subordinate has power to alter the composition of the labour force which is employed to achieve a given task. By employing a worker of a higher skill (and at a higher rate of pay) than that allowed for in the standard, the manager hopes to achieve an overall saving in labour cost. In our particular example, if this were the case, the action taken would not have been justified, since the higher rate of pay has not been offset by a greater gain in efficiency.

### Further analysis of the Efficiency Variance

It is often the case that the labour efficiency variance is more controllable than the wages rate variance, particularly by lower levels of management, who are usually more able to influence the time taken to do a job than the rate of pay. It may therefore be considered worth while keeping time records, which can reveal, in further detail, likely causes of the efficiency variance. For example, had there been an adverse efficiency variance, this could have been caused by idle time due to machine breakdown, idle time due to waiting for work, rework due to faulty material, or rework due to bad workmanship which did not pass inspection. Time records which permit further analysis under such headings can aid the manager in identifying the underlying causes of a variance; but even so, there may still be the need for further investigation, e.g. idle time due to waiting for work could be due to an understaffed production planning section, or simply due to inefficiency in the preceding section from which work is obtained.

### The Joint Variance

In the illustration given at Figure 50, one variance is favourable while the other is adverse. The other situation, where both variances are in the same direction, may be illustrated by the following set of figures (Figure 51).

|  | Actual | Standard | Variance |
|---|---|---|---|
| Hours | 5,400 | 5,000 | |
| Rate per hour | £4·50 | £4·00 | |
| Cost | £24,300 | £20,000 | £4,300 (adverse) |

Figure 51

Plotting these figures on a diagram, we obtain the result shown in Figure 52.

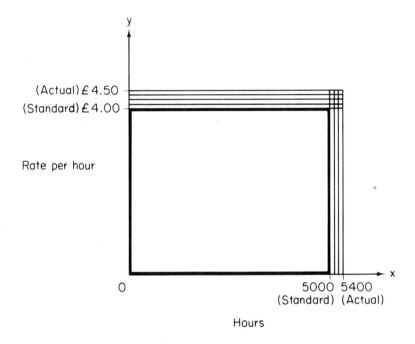

Figure 52

In this case, the labour force has taken more than standard time to carry out a certain amount of work, and has also cost more per hour than standard.

Both the efficiency and the rate variances are adverse, as can be seen by the shaded areas.

Although part of the excess can clearly be attributed to hours and part to rate, there is an area shaded . . . . . .

where it could be argued that the excess cost is due to both factors.

Rather than calculate a third, joint, variance, many accountants

would allocate the whole of this area to the rate variance, in which case
the diagram would appear as in Figure 53.

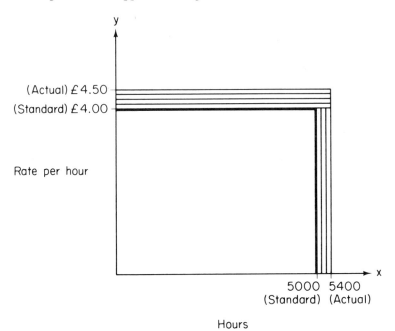

Figure 53


The variances are therefore as follows:

|  | £ |  |
|---|---|---|
| Labour efficiency variance | 1,600 | (adverse) |
| (400 hours × £4·00 per hour) | | |
| Wages rate variance | 2,700 | (adverse) |
| (50p per hour × 5,400 hours) | | |
| Wages cost variance | £4,300 | (adverse) |


The joint variance can also be found in connection with materials
variances.

## Materials Variances

Materials variances are calculated in a manner similar to labour variances, the analysis being based on quantities of materials and prices, instead of on labour hours and rates per hour. A materials usage variance corresponds to the labour efficiency variance in the previous calculation; and a materials price variance corresponds to the wages rate variance.

The calculation of these two materials variances may be illustrated by the set of figures relating to materials bought and used in production during a particular period shown in Figure 54.

|  | Actual | Standard | Variance |
|---|---|---|---|
| Quantity | 1,400 | 1,100 | |
| (units of material) | | | |
| Price per unit of material | £2 | £2·50 | |
| Cost | £2,800 | £2,750 | £50 (adverse) |

Figure 54

The £50 adverse materials cost variance has been found by comparing the actual materials cost incurred with the equivalent standard material cost. As in the case of the wages variance, analysis is needed in order to identify causes and the individual managers responsible for corrective action.

Let us consider the usage of materials first; actual quantity (1,400 units of material) exceeds standard quantity (1,100). This excess usage of 300 units is valued at the standard price per unit, £2·50, to produce an adverse materials usage variance of £750 (300 units × £2·50 per unit).

The adverse usage variance is largely offset by a favourable price variance: actual price (£2) is less than standard (£2·50), so that a saving of 50p per unit has been achieved on 1,400 units, making a favourable materials price variance of £700 (50p per unit × 1,400 units).

In summary:

|  | £ | |
|---|---|---|
| Materials usage variance | 750 | (adverse) |
| (300 units of material × £2·50 per unit) | | |
| Materials price variance | 700 | (favourable) |
| (50p per unit × 1,400 units of material) | | |
| Materials cost variance | £50 | (adverse) |

*Interpretation of Materials Variances*

In this example, variance analysis has highlighted a significant adverse usage variance which might otherwise have been hidden in the figures. The usage variance will generally be the responsibility of production management, whereas the price variance is more likely to be the responsibility of the buyer, so that one interpretation of the variances could be that production management should investigate the reasons for excess usage; while the buyer is to be congratulated on obtaining materials at a cheaper price than standard.

On the other hand, adverse usage might be related to adverse price, i.e. more units of a cheaper material may have been used in production. The materials usage variance may also be related to the labour efficiency variance: for example, inexperienced or inefficient labour may cause both labour efficiency and materials usage variances to be adverse. As noted in the previous sections, further investigations will usually be necessary in order to determine basic causes and an appropriate course of action.

Before leaving the subject of materials variances, it is perhaps worth noting that the accounting system may be designed to highlight the materials price variance either when the material is bought or when it is used. As the materials price variance is more likely to be the responsibility of the buyer, highlighting the variance at the point of purchase usually has the advantage. In the above example, the problem did not arise, because we assumed that the material was both bought and used in production during the same period.

*Overhead Variances—Expenditure*

In Chapter 2 we noted that the accountant can help managers, in the preparation of their departmental budgets, by analysing the behaviour of costs as the level of activity changes, so that costs which are likely to remain fixed in relation to a given variation in activity are separated from those which are likely to vary with that activity, and the rate of change of the latter is established. Given a particular planned level of activity, we noted that such an analysis should make it easier for managers to establish budgeted cost figures for their spheres of responsibility.

A knowledge of the behaviour of costs in relation to changes in the level of activity is also useful in comparing performance with plan, because it enables actual costs to be compared with budgeted costs, *at the level of activity actually achieved*. Without first adjusting budgeted figures, in order to bring them in line with actual levels of activity, a comparison between performance and plan might be misleading to management.

The point can be most clearly seen in a simple case, drawn from everyday life. Suppose that an individual draws up a budget for his car costs for the coming year, during which he budgets to motor 10,000 miles. He separates costs which are likely to remain fixed in relation to activity, i.e. in relation to mileage, from those which are likely to vary with mileage. Included in his budget are two headings—insurance (in the fixed category) and petrol (in the variable category). He budgets insurance cost at £400 for the coming year, and petrol at 6p per mile, the latter being based on an analysis of how petrol cost is likely to vary with mileage.

His budget will therefore include the headings in Figure 55.

|  | *Fixed* £ | *Variable* (pence per mile) | *Total* £ |
|---|---|---|---|
| Insurance | 400 | — | 400 |
| Petrol | — | 6p | 600* |

* 6p per mile × 10,000 miles

Figure 55

At the end of the year he measures his actual costs as follows: insurance £450, petrol £700; and compares these figures with budget.

|  | *Budget* £ | *Actual* £ | *Expenditure variance* £ |
|---|---|---|---|
| Insurance | 400 | 450 | 50 (adverse) |
| Petrol | 600* | 700 | 100 (adverse) |

* 6p per mile × 10,000 miles

Figure 56

Both insurance cost and petrol cost have exceeded budget, i.e. both cost headings show adverse expenditure variances. So far as the future control of petrol costs is concerned, it is clear that this comparison between budget and actual is meaningful only if the budgeted and actual levels of activity coincide: if the individual has in fact motored 10,000 miles during the year as planned. But if 12,500 miles have been covered instead, the expenditure variance on petrol means little, unless the budget is first adjusted. This adjustment has been made in the following set of figures.

|  | Original budget | Adjusted budget | Actual | Expenditure variance |
|---|---|---|---|---|
|  | £ | £ | £ | £ |
| Insurance | 400 | 400 | 450 | 50 (adverse) |
| Petrol | 600* | 750† | 700 | 50 (favourable) |

\* 6p per mile × 10,000 miles
† 6p per mile × 12,500 miles

Figure 57

The comparison between actual and adjusted budget now shows a favourable expenditure variance on petrol. The precise reason why this favourable expenditure has been achieved could be found by further investigation, as in previous illustrations: for example, it could be due to economical driving, or to a cut in the price of petrol. The essential point of the illustration is, however, that whenever costs are likely to vary with activity to any significant extent, a comparison between performance and plan has little meaning unless the budget is first adjusted to take account of the level of activity actually achieved. The technique of adjusting budgets in this way in known as variable budgeting.

Variable budgeting techniques can be applied to the preparation of reports for a wide variety of managers: in fact, whenever costs are likely to vary in response to changes in the level of activity. The technique is, of course, most frequently applied to reports for production managers, where several overhead costs may be found to vary to some extent with activity, including, for example, costs of power, consumable stores and repairs.

Expenditure variances, like the labour and materials cost variances considered in previous sections, are made up of quantity and price. Provided it were considered worth keeping the necessary records, and making the necessary calculations, it would be possible to split the various overhead expenditure variances into their quantity and price elements. For example, an adverse expenditure variance on consumable stores, appearing in a report for a production manager, could be analysed into the fraction due to the quantity used and the fraction due to the price of these stores. In many cases in practice, however, further analysis of this type is not undertaken, at least on a routine basis, because it is felt that managerial control is not materially assisted by the additional detail.

## Interpretation of Overhead Expenditure Variances

When interpreting overhead expenditure variances it is important to bear in mind the distinction between costs which can be pre-determined with a reasonable degree of certainty, given a level of activity, and items which are budgeted more by the exercise of managerial judgment. A number of overheads fall into the latter category, including, for example, many of the costs incurred in running the training, research and development, secretarial, legal, accounting and marketing departments. In such cases it is very difficult to say with any degree of certainty how much expenditure *should* be incurred at a particular level of activity, so that judgment has to be applied in deciding what work is to be done in the department in question, and what constitutes an efficient level of operations. Where the level of cost set in the budget, although carefully arrived at, is nevertheless at the discretion of management, a comparison between performance and plan becomes less a question of assessing efficiency against an independent yardstick, and more a question of ensuring that budgets are not exceeded without good reason.

Furthermore, a saving on budget may well prove to be a false economy with many of these discretionary costs. For example, a saving on inspection or on production planning in a factory may produce a favourable overhead expenditure variance, at the expense of adverse labour efficiency and materials usage variances in the future. In similar fashion, a saving on training, on research and development, or on the advertising budget, may prove to be detrimental to the company's efficiency and growth prospects in the long run. This is not, of course, to imply that once budgets for discretionary costs have been set, managers should not look for economies in operation; but it does mean that with discretionary costs a favourable expenditure variance is not necessarily a good thing; whereas with those overhead costs which can be predetermined with a reasonable degree of certainty, given a level of activity, a saving usually represents a useful economy in operation and an advantage to the company.

*Overhead Variances—Volume*

Changes in the level of activity affect accounting for fixed overheads in a particular way. As we saw in Chapter 4, changes in volume can result in differing costs per unit of product, because the same fixed overheads are being spread over a greater or lesser number of units. We also noted that a system could be adopted whereby fixed overheads could be charged to units of product at a standard rate. For example, we might charge fixed overheads on the basis of £0·50 per unit of product, based on a budgeted volume of 1,000 units and a budgeted fixed overhead of £500. If the actual volume of production differs from budget, too much or too little overhead will have been charged to production, and this excess or deficiency can be reported by the accountant as a volume variance.

Suppose, for example, that actual volume during a particular period was 800 units of product. Production would therefore be charged with fixed overhead amounting to £400 (800 units × the standard rate of £0·50 per unit). This is £100 less than the amount of fixed overhead budgeted for, so that the accountant can report an adverse volume variance of £100. This is the measure by which fixed overhead has not been recovered in production, due to the actual volume of production falling below the budgeted level.

Instead of charging overhead at an amount per unit of product, it is possible to charge so much per standard hour. The standard hour is a useful common denominator for summing up the volume of production of several products, which would otherwise be expressed in dissimilar units.

Suppose that a company makes two products, A and B, and that 1 unit of product A should take one hour to complete and 1 unit of product B should take half an hour to complete. These are the standard times set for standard costing purposes. A budgeted production of 500 units of A and 1,000 units of B would therefore represent 1,000 standard hours of work (500 × 1 standard hour) + (1,000 × ½ standard hour). Assuming that the budgeted fixed overhead is £500, fixed overhead in this case will be charged to production at the rate of £0·50 per standard hour (£500 ÷ 1,000 standard hours).

If actual production consists of 400 units of A and 900 units of B, this may be expressed in equivalent standard hours as follows:

A: 400 units × 1 standard hour per unit = 400 standard hours
B: 900 units × ½ standard hour per unit = 450 standard hours

Total production    850 standard hours

In this case the amount charged to production for fixed overhead will be 850 standard hours × £0·50 per standard hour = £425. This is £75 less than the £500 budgeted for, so that there is an adverse volume variance of £75, which, again, is the measure by which fixed overhead has not been recovered in production, due to the actual volume of production falling below the budgeted level.

*Interpretation and Further Analysis of Overhead Volume Variances*

Differences between budgeted and actual volumes of production may arise for a number of reasons, some controllable, others not, including such reasons as machine breakdown, bottlenecks in the works, or lack of orders. Even lack of orders may be controllable in the sense that the marketing department could perhaps have been more vigorous in obtaining the required share of the market. Problems will therefore arise in the interpretation of the volume variance because of the wide variety of causes which may be operative, and the possibility that several managers may be involved, each taking part responsibility for the necessary corrective action. As in previous illustrations, further analysis may be carried out by the accountant in order to present managers with more detailed variances, analysed by cause, which may help to narrow the field of enquiry.

One such analysis is to separate the influence of efficiency of working from capacity utilization: a distinction may be made between volume variances which arise because people produce more or less than is expected of them during a given period of time, and those which arise because people work longer or shorter hours than planned. The former variance, the productivity variance, measures the extent to which overhead is either over- or under-recoevered because the labour force has either bettered or failed to achieve the standard times set. The point of making this separation is that lower levels of management may be able to control the speed of working, and hence the productivity variance; whereas they may be less able to influence the capacity variance, which arises when the labour force is at work for longer or shorter periods of time than planned.

One other obvious reason why a volume variance can arise is that the number of working hours available in a particular period has differed from the budgeted figure, e.g. due to a holiday which was not allowed for in drawing up the budget, so that it might also be helpful to isolate this influence on overhead recovery by means of a calendar variance.

These variances are a useful beginning to finding out why actual volume has differed from budget: they focus managers' attention on important aspects of the situation. Nevertheless, a large number of influences will have affected volume, so that the problem of isolating basic causes, and identifying the necessary corrective action, may well prove to be difficult, and will often require further investigation beyond accounting analysis.

*Sales Variances*

A useful set of sales variances may be calculated, showing the effect of differences between budgeted and actual sales quantities; the budgeted and actual mix of products sold; and budgeted and actual sales prices. These variances help to explain why the income, or profit, from sales has exceeded or fallen below budget. They may be illustrated by the following set of figures, which assume that two products, A and B, are sold.

| | Qty (units) | | Sales Mix | Sales Price £ | Sales Income £ | |
|---|---|---|---|---|---|---|
| | | BUDGETED SALES | | | | |
| A | 30 | | $\frac{1}{4}$ | 10 | 300 | |
| B | 90 | } 120 | $\frac{3}{4}$ | 12 | 1080 | £1380 |
| | | ACTUAL SALES | | | | |
| | Qty (units) | | Sales Mix | Sales Price £ | Sales Income £ | |
| A | 40 | | $\frac{2}{5}$ | 9 | 360 | |
| B | 60 | } 100 | $\frac{3}{5}$ | 13 | 780 | £1140 |
| | | | | Sales variance | £ 240 | (adverse) |

Figure 58

Sales income has fallen below budget to the extent of £240. A preliminary survey of the figures indicates three factors at work: the total quantity sold is 20 units below budget; the proportion which each product bears to the total, i.e. the sales mix, has altered from $\frac{1}{4}$ A, $\frac{3}{4}$ B, to $\frac{2}{5}$ A, $\frac{3}{5}$ B; and sales prices have also been changed, from £10 A, £12 B, to £9 A, £13 B.

Each of these factors represents a fraction of the £240 adverse sales variance as shown in Figure 59.

| | | | | (A)=Adverse |  |  |
|---|---|---|---|---|---|---|
| | | | | VARIANCES (F)=Favourable | | |
| Qty (units) | Sales Mix | Sales Price | Sales Income | Qty | Mix | Price |
| | | £ | £ | £ | £ | £ |

*Stage 1. As Budgeted*

| | | | | |
|---|---|---|---|---|
| 120 × | $\frac{1}{4}$ × | 10 = | 300 |
| 120 × | $\frac{3}{4}$ × | 12 = | 1080 |
| | | | £1380 | — — — |

The budgeted figures are the starting point from which differences between budget and actual will be analysed.

*Stage 2. Total Qty 100 units*

| | | | | |
|---|---|---|---|---|
| 100 × | $\frac{1}{4}$ × | 10 = | 250 |
| 100 × | $\frac{3}{4}$ × | 12 = | 900 |
| | | | £1150 | £230(A) — — |

The difference between the budgeted and actual total quantity is the first to be analysed. This difference, taken in isolation, results in an adverse variance of £230 (£1,150—£1,380).

*Stage 3. Sales Mix A $\frac{2}{5}$, B $\frac{3}{5}$*

| | | | | |
|---|---|---|---|---|
| 100 × | $\frac{2}{5}$ × | 10 = | 400 |
| 100 × | $\frac{3}{5}$ × | 12 = | 720 |
| | | | £1120 | — £30 (A) — |

This stage isolates the effect of a change in mix from $\frac{1}{4}$ A, $\frac{3}{4}$ B, to $\frac{2}{5}$ A, $\frac{3}{5}$ B, resulting in a further adverse variance of £30 (£1120—£1150).

*Stage 4. Sales Prices A £9, B £13*

| 100 | × | $\frac{2}{5}$ | × | 9 = | 360 | | |
|---|---|---|---|---|---|---|---|
| 100 | × | $\frac{3}{5}$ | × | 13 = | 780 | | |

£1140 — — £20 (F)

This stage completes the analysis, by isolating the further effect of a change in sales prices from £10 A, £12 B to £9 A, £13 B, resulting in a favourable variance of £20 (£1140—£1120).

SUMMARY

| | £ | |
|---|---|---|
| Quantity variance | 230 | (adverse) |
| Mix variance | 30 | (adverse) |
| Price variance | 20 | (favourable) |
| Sales variance | £240 | (adverse) |

Figure 59

*Interpretation and Further Analysis of Sales Variances*

The three variances separated in Figure 59 explain the overall difference between budgeted and actual sales, in terms of loss of income, and show the reason is mainly because the total quantity sold has fallen below budget; and to a much lesser extent because more of A and less of B has been sold; offset to some extent by a revision in prices, B being sold at a higher price than budgeted and A at a lower price. The mix and price variances could, of course, be inter-related, i.e. it is possible that more of A was sold because of the price cut on A; and less of B because of the price increase. Because of the many factors at work in the market affecting sales figures, such an analysis, although valuable, is obviously again only a beginning to an understanding of the reasons why sales income has differed from budget.

By using standard gross profit per unit instead of sales price in the above calculation, the figures could be reworked to show the effect of quantity and mix variances on profit (the price variance will, of course, have the same effect on both income and profit).

An analysis which shows the effect of sales variances on profit is particularly valuable where different products carry different gross profit margins and where, for example, a change in mix could have serious profit consequences which need highlighting, if the swing is away from products which earn high gross profit margins towards products which earn lower margins.

*Further Comparisons between Performance and Plan*

Provided the necessary records have been kept and the information is felt to be a useful aid to management, comparisons may be made between performance and plan extending beyond those relating to labour, materials, overheads and sales, as have been outlined in this chapter. For example, mix variances may also be calculated to show the effect on costs of differences between the standard and actual composition of the labour force or between the standard and actual composition of the materials used in production.

Comparisons between performance and plan may also be made relating to assets: for example, a comparison may be made between actual and budgeted stock levels, or between the actual and budgeted cash, debtor and creditor levels. Ratios, such as those outlined in Chapter 1, may also be used as a means of reporting some of these comparisons.

Comparisons may also be made in connection with individual jobs or contracts, or in connection with capital projects, to ensure that estimates of expenditure are not exceeded; and in the latter case, as noted in Chapter 3, it may also be possible to carry out post-audits to see whether the projects have yielded their expected benefits, e.g. in the form of extra cash flow or in the form of cost savings. The variety of reports which could be provided is obviously considerable, and will depend upon the circumstances of individual businesses and the information needs of individual managers, but all such reports should be designed as a useful aid to management, in the sense that they should aid decision making in the control of performance, or in the re-appraisal of plans, or in the improvement of planning in the future.

*Summary*

In this chapter we have seen how the accountant can aid managers by reporting on, and analysing, important variances between performance and plan. These variances have been considered under two main headings: cost variances and sales variances. The cost variances were divided into those relating to labour time and rates of pay, those relating to materials usage and price, and those relating to overheads. In connection with overheads, the important technique of variable budgeting was explained, whereby budgets are adjusted to correspond with the level of activity actually achieved, before comparisons are made and expenditure variances reported. The effect of volume on the recovery of fixed overheads was also explained, which led to a consideration of the effect on overhead recovery of changes in the productivity of working and changes in capacity utilization. Sales variances were considered under three main headings: those relating to quantity, mix and price, and it was noted that such variances could report the effect of each of these factors either on sales income or on profits. Finally, other important comparisons between performance and plan were outlined. Throughout the chapter attention has been paid to the interpretation of the figures presented; the recognition of important interrelationships between variances; and the frequent need for further investigations before corrective action can be taken.

# 6 MANAGEMENT AND CHANGE

Managers work in an environment of change. In this chapter we discuss how accounting can provide a clearer insight into the likely effects of change, whether it arises from market forces or is deliberately created by managers themselves. This is a continuation of a theme which has run throughout previous chapters, and leads us to consider further aspects of volume, price, cost and product-mix changes, including a discussion of the use of break-even charts, marginal costing statements and accounting information generally, in the solution of problems of alternative choice. We begin by considering cost behaviour in relation to changes in the level of activity, so that our attention is directed first to the problem of isolating fixed and variable costs.

*Cost Behaviour and the Level of Activity*

The analysis of costs into fixed or variable in relation to changes in the level of activity can only be carried out according to the facts of particular cases. Statements that certain costs are fixed or variable should always be related to the underlying circumstances, so that a cost item is not fixed or variable as such, but because it has been found upon investigation to be so *in a particular case*. With this proviso in mind, we can nevertheless say that certain cost items tend, by their nature, to fall more frequently into one category than the other.

*Fixed Costs*

Factory rent, management salaries, depreciation of plant and equipment, for example, are more likely to be classified as fixed than variable, because the range of activity within which such costs remain unchanged is fairly wide. If an investigation of a particular case shows that certain costs are likely to remain fixed in this way, they may be represented graphically as shown in Figure 60. Costs are plotted along the *y*-axis and activity along the *x*-axis, and because the costs are considered to remain constant over the range of activity plotted, the graph line is drawn parallel to the *x*-axis.

*Variable Costs*

Certain costs such as materials are classified as variable with changes in the level of activity. Direct labour may also be classed as a variable

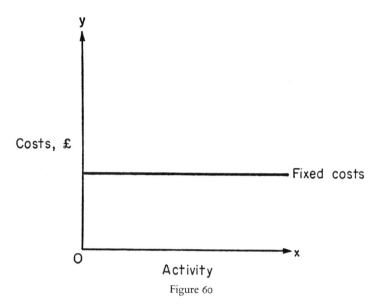

Figure 60

cost, although there will be situations where labour costs exhibit a degree of fixity, especially following a reduction in the level of activity.

If we make the assumption that variable costs move in a straight line over the range of activity we are plotting, these costs may be repre-

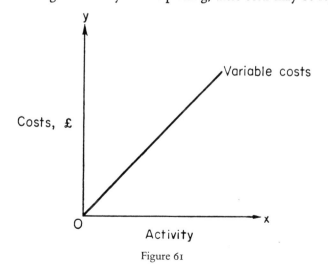

Figure 61

sented graphically as in Figure 61, with zero cost at zero activity, and a progressive rise in cost as activity rises.

(The validity of the straight-line assumptions which we are making in these illustrations will be discussed later in the chapter.)

### Semi-Fixed Costs

Many costs do not fall neatly into the categories of fixed or variable. They contain an element of both and are known as semi-fixed or semi-variable costs. An example of such a cost (which we will call semi-fixed) is the cost of telephones. Telephone charges are made up of a fixed cost element, the rental, which is incurred regardless of the number of calls made; and a variable cost element, the cost of calls, which will tend to vary as activity varies. Such a cost may be represented graphically as in Figure 62, which shows the fixed cost element

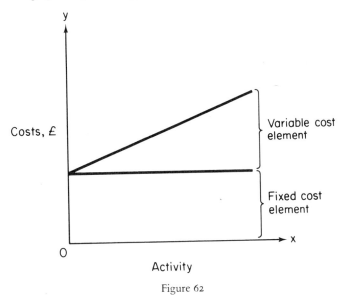

Figure 62

incurred at zero activity, with the variable cost element rising as activity rises.

Repairs and maintenance to plant is another example of a semi-fixed cost. A certain amount of maintenance work will usually be necessary, even though the plant is not used (oiling, greasing, cleaning etc.); whereas, once plant is used, the repairs and maintenance cost will probably rise. In this case, however, it may not be possible to identify readily the fixed cost element in the total cost.

*Scatter Charts*

Statistical devices may be employed by the accountant to separate the fixed and variable elements in such a semi-fixed cost. One commonly found device is a scatter chart, on which costs are plotted against activity. Figure 63 is an illustration of a scatter chart for an assumed

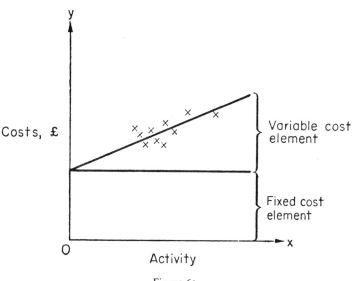

Figure 63

case of repairs and maintenance cost; each plot on the graph represents one recorded or estimated relationship between costs and activity.

Having created sufficient plottings to obtain a pattern, a line of best fit is drawn through the scatter (the line may be derived by mathematical techniques or simply drawn by visual inspection). This line of best fit need not actually cut through any of the plottings, but it is drawn so as best to represent them all. The line is continued back to the $y$-axis, and the level of cost where it cuts the $y$-axis is considered to be the fixed cost element. The variable cost element at each level of activity and the fixed cost element can then be read separately from the chart. The rate of change of the variable cost element can, of course, be found by measuring the increase in variable cost following a given increase in activity.

The scatter-chart/line-of-best-fit approach is not the only way of attempting to isolate the fixed and variable cost elements in a semi-fixed cost; but other methods, in common with the one illustrated, will all produce approximate results. This approximation is a point for managers to bear in mind when using accounting reports based on a distinction between fixed and variable costs.

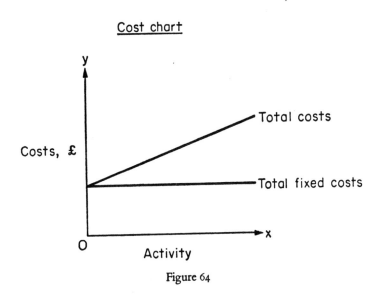

Figure 64

*Cost Chart*

On the assumption that a fixed and variable cost analysis has been undertaken for the various costs incurred by a business, the accountant is in a position to summarize the figures into two categories: total fixed costs, and total variable costs. The total fixed costs will consist of those items which were initially classified as fixed, together with the fixed cost elements separated from the semi-fixed costs. Similarly, the total variable costs will consist of those costs initially classified as variable, together with the variable cost elements separated from the semi-fixed costs at each level of activity. These figures may be plotted on a cost chart such as Figure 64, where the total variable costs are plotted on top of the total fixed, so that the upper line shows the total costs which are likely to be incurred by the business at different levels of activity.

*Break-even Chart*

A cost chart, such as the one at Figure 64, is the basis for a break-even chart. A break-even chart is created by drawing a third line, the sales line, using the *y*-axis to plot sales as well as costs. Figure 65 shows a break-even chart with activity measured in terms of units of output (there are, of course, several alternative ways of measuring activity which will be outlined later in the chapter). The sales line in Figure 65 shows the revenue from selling various units of output.

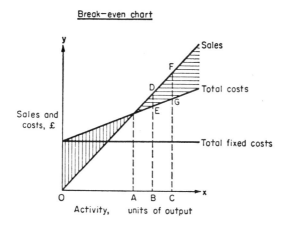

Figure 65

The point where the sales line cuts the total costs line is the break-even point for the business: the point of no profit, no loss. The break-even level of activity can be read off the *x*-axis, OA units in Figure 65.

Above the break-even point profits are made, as indicated by the profit zone shaded . . . . . .

where the revenue from sales exceeds total costs. Below the break-even point losses are incurred, as indicated by the loss zone shaded . . . . . .  where total costs exceed the revenue from sales.

At the present level of activity, which we will assume is measured by the distance OB on the chart, we can read off the likely profit to be earned if this level of activity continues. The likely profit is measured by the distance DE.

The break-even chart also shows the difference between the present level of activity and the break-even level. This difference, AB, is known as the margin of safety, and is the amount by which activity could fall back from the present level before losses are incurred. This margin is a further factor in the assessment of the economic strength of a business and is complementary to the various ratios outlined in Chapter 1. Every business will experience some fluctuation in activity, due for example to the influence of competitors and changes in market conditions, and the margin of safety is a measure of the ability of the business to ride out these ups and downs of trade without incurring losses.

It is also possible to obtain from the break-even chart a visual impression of the profit potential from expansion. If, for example, output is expanded from OB to OC units in Figure 65, the chart shows the likely rise in profit, from DE to FG. The amount by which profit changes, following a given change in activity, will obviously depend upon the width of the angle between the sales and the total costs lines: the wider the angle, the greater the change.

*Uses of the Break-Even Chart*

Because the break-even chart brings together sales revenue and total costs on one diagram, it can be used to assess the likely effects of changes under either or both of these headings. Because sales revenue is made up of volume and sales price, and total costs are classified into fixed or variable, changes in any one of these factors, or combinations in these factors, may also be studied. The chart is therefore a useful device for focusing attention on certain key factors in a business, and the relationships between them.

*Change in Volume*

We have already seen how the chart may be used to show the likely effect of a change in volume, e.g. in Figure 65 an increase from OB to OC units, with a consequent increase in profit and margin of safety.

*Change in Sales Price*

In Figure 66, the effect of a change in sales price is shown, where a price cut has been assumed and a new sales line has therefore been drawn at a flatter angle to the *x*-axis.

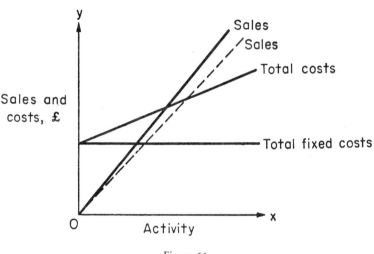

**Effect of change in sales price**

Figure 66

Figure 66 shows that the price cut will raise the break-even point of the business and correspondingly lower the margin of safety. Because the angle between the sales and total cost lines has flattened, the price cut will also have the effect of altering the amount by which profit changes following a given change in activity. Of course a key question in the case of a price cut is its likely effect on the volume of sales, and hence on the level of activity of the business. This is obviously not a question which the accountant can answer, but is a matter for the marketing manager, who must assess such factors as the price-consciousness of the market and the possible reactions of competitors to the price cut.

Important factors which *can* be read from the break-even chart, however, are the extent to which activity must increase simply in order to recover the original profit position; and the likely profit to be earned at various alternative levels of activity, several of which might be the consequence of the price cut.

### Change in Fixed Costs

The effect of an increase in total fixed costs, and hence in total costs, resulting for example from a proposal to increase an administrative department, can be seen in Figure 67 (where only total costs and sales are plotted). The effect is an initial fall in profit, an increase in break-even point, and a corresponding fall in the margin of safety; but no change in the amount by which profit rises or falls following a given change in activity, because the angle between the sales and total-costs lines remains the same.

### Effect of change in fixed costs

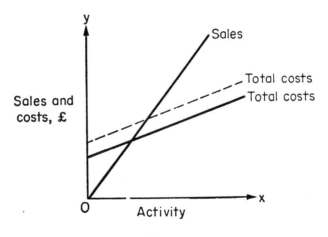

Figure 67

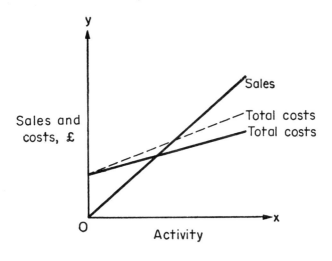

Figure 68

*Change in Variable Costs*

In similar fashion, the effect of an increase in total variable costs, and hence in total costs, due for example to an increase in raw material prices, may be seen in Figure 68 (where, again, only total costs and sales are plotted). The effect in this case is a fall in profit; an increase in break-even point, and a corresponding fall in the margin of safety; *and* a change in the amount by which profit rises or falls following a given change in the level of activity, due to the narrowing of the angle between the sales and total-costs lines.

*Activity Measures*

In Figure 65, activity was measured in terms of units of output, but alternative ways of measuring activity might also have been adopted. Basically, the choice is between a measure related to output, or one related to input. There is also the choice between measurement in non-money or in money terms. Some alternative measures to units of output are: numbers of units sold; sales value of units sold; standard hours produced (the standard-hours equivalent of the number of units produced); actual hours worked (labour or machine hours); percentage of capacity utilized (capacity often being defined in terms of an hours basis). Measures of activity based on hours or value have the advantage of enabling charts to be drawn for multi-product situations, where the various products, normally measured in dissimilar units, e.g. bottles, ounces, packs, can be expressed in terms of a common denominator.

### Factors Affecting the Interpretation of a Break-Even Chart

We have already seen that a break-even chart depends upon a preliminary analysis of the behaviour of costs, which is approximate in nature, so that a break-even chart does not give a precise measurement of what will happen to costs at various levels of activity, but is more an indicator of what is expected to happen under a variety of assumptions regarding the behaviour of costs. In addition, several other factors should be borne in mind when interpreting a break-even chart.

1. *The question of whether the chart is up to date.* The chart is a model, representing the cost structure and pricing policy of a business, and if any significant change takes place in these underlying factors, the chart may need to be redrawn.

2. *The question of changes in product mix.* Where a chart relates to a multi-product situation, and the various products are sold at different prices and incur different costs, a change in the mix of products made and sold might mean that the original lines on the chart need to be redrawn.

3. *The question of the straight-line assumption.* Although the use of straight lines is usually considered acceptable in practice, particularly if there is a tendency in combining several cost items into one graph line for variations to cancel each other out, the use of straight lines carries with it the strong possibility that the chart may not be valid over the whole range of activity shown. For example, total fixed costs will almost certainly step up at intervals over the whole range; and over a wide range of activity the total cost line could slope to a significant extent, because of disproportionate changes in variable costs. It is important therefore for the manager to be sure

of the range of activity within which the chart is reasonably valid: a restricted range where fixed costs, for all practical purposes, may be regarded as fixed, and variable costs, for all practical purposes, may be held to behave in a linear fashion. Such a restriction does not necessarily render the chart less useful to the manager, as he is likely to be primarily interested in a relatively narrow range, the practicable alternative range of activity around the present level, rather than in the whole range of activity shown on the chart.

4. *The use of direct costing principles.* In Chapter 4 we saw how different profit and loss figures could be obtained by the use of direct-costing and full-costing principles, and that these differences only arose when there was a build-up or run-down of stocks, i.e. when sales and output were out of balance. The break-even chart calculates profit in line with direct-costing principles, and the profit shown on the chart need not agree with the profit shown in the profit and loss account. It will not do so if the latter has been drawn up on full-costing principles and sales and output are out of balance.

Despite these aspects affecting interpretation, the break-even chart is a useful indicator for managers; one of its particular features being the readily understandable form in which it presents key factors affecting profit. By considering the implications of a proposal in terms of likely changes in profit, break-even point and margin of safety, not only is a framework provided for analysis, but the analysis itself is likely to be more searching as a result.

*Marginal Costing and Contribution*

One of the points raised in connection with the break-even chart was that changes in the mix of products made and sold might invalidate the lines drawn on the chart. It would, of course, be possible to prepare several charts to show the effect of selling various combinations of products, but as an alternative, schedules could be drawn up on a marginal costing basis.

As an illustration of the marginal cost approach, suppose that a company sells three products, A, B and C. A study of the costs incurred in making and selling these products indicates that some costs are likely to vary, if the quantity made and sold is varied; while other costs are likely to remain fixed within the likely alternative ranges of activity. A schedule is prepared (Figure 69) showing the sales revenue and the variable costs associated with each product, and the contribution which each product is estimated to make towards the total fixed costs and profit of the business.

PRODUCTS

| | A<br>£'000 | B<br>£'000 | C<br>£'000 | Total<br>£'000 | |
|---|---|---|---|---|---|
| Sales | 60 | 110 | 200 | 370 | |
| Variable costs | 25 | 35 | 70 | 130 | |
| Contribution | 35 | 75 | 130 | 240 | |
| Total fixed costs | | | | 200 | |
| Profit | | | | £40 | =approx. 11%<br>of sales. |

Figure 69

Product A is estimated to contribute £35,000, product B £75,000 and product C £130,000 towards the total fixed costs and profits of the business. The total of these contributions, £240,000, is enough to cover the total fixed costs, £200,000, and leave an overall profit of £40,000. The overall profit margin is approximately 11% of sales.

This form of presentation enables a manager to see clearly the profit consequences of changes in the sales mix. For example, suppose that a 20% increase in the sales of A is under consideration, i.e. an increase to £72,000. Variable costs associated with A will, as a consequence, rise by 20% to £30,000. Assuming, for simplicity, that no other changes are foreseen, the schedule will now appear as in **Figure 70 overleaf**.

The result of this particular change in sales mix is that the overall profit of the company will rise from £40,000 to £47,000, with an increase in profit margin from approximately 11% to approximately 12% of sales. Similar calculations could be prepared for other possible changes in mix, including simultaneous changes, e.g. where the sales of one product are considered to have an effect on the sales of another.

PRODUCTS

|  | A £'000 | B £'000 | C £'000 | Total £'000 |  |
|---|---|---|---|---|---|
| Sales | 72 | 110 | 200 | 382 | |
| Variable costs | 30 | 35 | 70 | 135 | |
| Contribution | 42 | 75 | 130 | 247 | |
| Total fixed costs | | | | 200 | |
| Profit | | | | £47 | =approx. 12% of sales. |

Figure 70

*Contribution per Unit*

As a further aid to decision making, it is helpful to know, for each product separately, the contribution to be obtained from a given increase in volume. This can help managers to establish a sales-mix policy by ranking products in order of priority from a contribution viewpoint.

Figure 71 shows the contribution per unit sold, for products A, B and C, on the assumption that the number of units sold are: A 60,000 units, B 100,000 units, C 200,000 units.

PRODUCTS

|  | A | B | C |
|---|---|---|---|
| Contribution | £42,000 | £75,000 | £130,000 |
| No of units sold | 60,000 | 100,000 | 200,000 |
| Contribution per unit sold | £0·70 | £0·75 | £0·65 |

Figure 71

Figure 71 clearly ranks the products in order of preference, B, A, C, from the point of view of the contribution to be obtained from selling one more unit. Such a report is therefore a useful aid in determining sales policy and the priorities to be accorded to different lines. The analysis is not, of course, sufficient in itself, as it leaves out of account marketing considerations affecting sales mix, such as the market potential for each product and the effect on customer goodwill of altering the range of products offered for sale.

The contribution approach may also be adopted when factors other than sales are likely to limit the scale of operations. For example, the available supply of materials, labour or machine capacity could each limit the scale of operations for a particular period. During this period it might be considered worthwhile changing the mix of products, in order to concentrate on those which yield the highest contribution per unit of limiting factor used up, e.g. per unit of material used, or per labour or machine hour occupied.

*Contribution Pricing*

The contribution approach is also useful in setting selling prices in certain situations. While it is evident that managers must aim to earn sufficient sales revenue to cover *all* costs and earn an acceptable rate of profit, there may be situations where it is reasonable to sell individual products at a price which is in excess of variable cost only, with the result that the product makes some contribution to the fixed costs of the business.

Such a practice might be justified, for example, if a business had spare capacity which might otherwise lie idle, so that additional business might be accepted, provided it made a contribution to fixed costs. In similar fashion, an existing product might be retained, provided it made a contribution—and provided no better alternative product could be found—because by dropping the product the contribution would be lost, and some contribution to fixed costs is better than none at all.

Contribution pricing involves many considerations which are outside accounting. For example, the possibility that a contribution price will spoil the market for existing business, or that repeat orders of special business will also be negotiated on this basis; or the possibility that more profitable business may have to be foregone in the future, because capacity has been absorbed on marginal business. On the other hand, there is the possibility that a low price for a product may stimulate demand and provide a long-run profitable result, by offering the opportunity of more efficient working at higher volumes. Furthermore, a low price on one product may stimulate the sales of another, particularly if they are complimentary in use, e.g. razors and razor blades.

Nevertheless, it should be emphasized that a business survives only if it earns, in total, a sufficient contribution to cover its fixed costs and make an acceptable profit; for this reason, therefore, contribution pricing should be used with caution, and is more often appropriate to short-term situations, where the emphasis is on making the best use of available resources, than for long-term pricing decisions.

*Relevant Figures*

A feature of the marginal cost approach is the selection of those revenues and costs which are relevant to the problem under consideration. The product-mix illustrations, for example, involved changes in sales revenue and variable costs only, so that attention was focused primarily on those elements in the profit equation.

The identification of relevant figures is fundamental to an analysis of all problems of alternative choice, such as whether to keep or drop a product; whether to accept or decline additional business; whether to make or buy a component; whether to change the method of working, etc. Each case will require separate consideration by the manager and the accountant jointly, to identify the possible alternative courses of action and to identify the figure consequences of these alternatives.

In considering problems of alternative choice involving a classification of costs into fixed and variable, it is important to note that existing classifications should not be used without further examination. As we noted at the beginning of the chapter, statements that certain costs are fixed or variable should always be related to the underlying circumstances of the case, so that a cost item is not fixed or variable as such, but because it has been found, upon investigation, to be so *in a particular case*. The extent of the particular change contemplated in an alternative choice problem, and the permanency of the change, are but two of the reasons why existing classifications of cost may no longer apply. In fact caution should always be exercised when drawing on existing accounting information, because it may be designed for a different purpose to the one in hand, or it may be based on assumptions which no longer hold good. The net result is that problems of alternative choice generally require the preparation of a special report outside the normal flow of accounting information.

*Summary*

In this chapter we have developed the theme of change. Changes in the level of activity and consequent changes in costs were discussed first, including the division of costs into fixed, variable and semi-fixed, and the analysis of the latter into their fixed and variable elements. Scatter charts and cost charts were explained, leading to the break-even chart. The break-even chart was seen to be a useful form of presentation, which could be used by managers to consider changes in volume, sales prices, fixed costs and variable costs, or combinations of these factors, particularly as they affect profit, break-even point and margin of safety. Marginal costing was illustrated by reference to sales-mix problems, using the concept of contribution per unit of product sold, and contribution per unit of other limiting factors. Contribution pricing was also discussed and its uses and dangers noted. Finally, it was emphasized that problems of alternative choice require a careful selection of relevant figures, and that this usually requires the preparation of a special accounting report outside the normal flow of accounting information.

An appendix to this chapter contains illustrations and brief descriptions of two alternative forms of graphical presentation of volume, price and cost relationships.

*Appendix to Chapter 6*

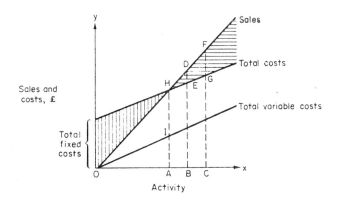

Figure 72

This alternative form of presentation shows the total variable costs, and plots the total fixed costs on top to produce the total costs line. As in previous illustrations, the chart shows the break-even point, margin of safety, profit and change in profit following a change in activity. Readers should compare Figure 65 with Figure 72 in this respect. The additional feature of Figure 72 is that it clearly shows how the total contribution (sales minus total variable costs) gradually increases, until it equals the total fixed costs (the distance HI) at the break-even level of activity. Thereafter, the total contribution exceeds the total fixed costs so that a profit is earned.

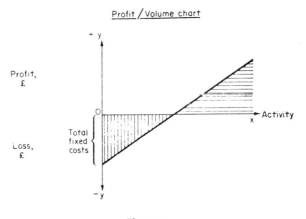

Figure 73

This is a simplified version of a break-even chart. Instead of plotting sales and cost lines separately, one line is drawn showing the total profit or loss at various levels of activity. The line is drawn from the *y*-axis at a distance below the zero equal to the total fixed costs.

Up to the point where the line cuts the *x*-axis, losses are incurred as indicated by the area shaded . . . . .

The point of intersection with the activity line is the break-even point. Thereafter profits are earned, as indicated by the area shaded . . . . . .

# INDEX